Teaching Reading and Literature with Classroom Talk

Dialogical Approaches and Practical Strategies in the Secondary ELA Classroom

Dawan Coombs

Routledge
Taylor & Francis Group

NEW YORK AND LONDON

Designed cover image: © Getty Images

First published 2025
by Routledge
605 Third Avenue, New York, NY 10158

and by Routledge
4 Park Square, Milton Park, Abingdon, Oxon, OX14 4RN

Routledge is an imprint of the Taylor & Francis Group, an informa business

© 2025 Dawan Coombs

The right of Dawan Coombs to be identified as author of this work has been asserted in accordance with sections 77 and 78 of the Copyright, Designs and Patents Act 1988.

All rights reserved. No part of this book may be reprinted or reproduced or utilised in any form or by any electronic, mechanical, or other means, now known or hereafter invented, including photocopying and recording, or in any information storage or retrieval system, without permission in writing from the publishers.

Trademark notice: Product or corporate names may be trademarks or registered trademarks, and are used only for identification and explanation without intent to infringe.

ISBN: 978-1-032-73949-6 (hbk)
ISBN: 978-1-032-73627-3 (pbk)
ISBN: 978-1-003-46684-0 (ebk)

DOI: 10.4324/9781003466840

Typeset in Palatino
by SPi Technologies India Pvt Ltd (Straive)

Teaching Reading and Literature with Classroom Talk

This book presents a framework for conceptualizing and enacting dialogic approaches to teaching literature and reading in your classroom. Dialogical approaches have often been used in secondary classrooms for teaching writing by incorporating students' lives and experiences into the English Language Arts (ELA) curriculum. But what might it look like to create reading moments that bring texts to life by allowing students to use their own identities and experiences as the foundation for their interpretation? The most current research in reading, motivation, culturally responsive teaching, and even neuroscience points to the power of dialogical approaches to not only engage students in reading texts, but also—when used consistently and repeatedly—help increase students' reading growth and achievement. Dialogical approaches can be particularly helpful for struggling readers, English language learners (ELLs), and neurodivergent students. This book explores dialogical approaches to teaching reading and literature in secondary ELA classrooms with descriptions of hands-on activities, models of dialogical strategies, and real-time examples from ELA and reading classes. Each chapter includes motivating, accessible, and research-based methods and tools that help students connect content to their lives and explore a diversity of perspectives. With resources such as assignment sheets and rubrics, this is an essential book for middle and high school ELA teachers, reading coaches and interventionists, teachers working with ELLs, and pre-service teachers who are looking to better understand and utilize dialogical approaches to support their students in transforming their reader identities.

Dawan Coombs is Associate Professor of English at Brigham Young University, USA.

Also Available from Routledge Eye On Education
(www.routledge.com/eyeoneducation)

The Antiracist English Language Arts Classroom
Keisha Rembert

Grammar Inquiries, Grades 6–12: An Inquiry- and Asset-Based Approach to Grammar Instruction
Sean Ruday

Teaching with Hip Hop in the 7–12 Grade Classroom: A Guide to Supporting Students' Critical Development Through Popular Texts
Lauren Kelly

The Literacy Coaching Handbook: Working With Teachers to Increase Student Achievement, 2nd edition
Diana Sisson and Betsy Sisson

Teach This Poem, Volume I: The Natural World
Madeleine Fuchs Holzer and The Academy of American Poets

Student-Centered Literacy Assessment in the 6–12 Classroom: An Asset-Based Approach
Sean Ruday and Katie Caprino

Bolstering Vocabulary with Teacher Talk in the Classroom: Strategic Modeling to Elevate Students' Language
Kristen Haase and Carmen Shahadi Rowe

Teaching Reading and Literature with Classroom Talk: Dialogical Approaches and Practical Strategies in the Secondary ELA Classroom
Dawan Coombs

Dedication

for mom, dad, and all the Travises

Contents

Meet the Author . . . . *viii*
Acknowledgments. . . . . *ix*
Foreword. . . . .*x*
Bob Fecho

1 **Exploring a Dialogical Approach to Teaching Literature** 1

2 **Artifactual Inquiries**. 33

3 **Simulations** 67

4 **Drama** 100

5 **Integrating Dialogical Approaches** .133

6 **Continuing the Dialogue**. 179

Appendix: Texts Mentioned 195

Meet the Author

Dawan Coombs is a former high school English and reading teacher who works as an Associate Professor of English at Brigham Young University, where she teaches courses in reading pedagogy and young adult literature. Her research examines pedagogies that support adolescent readers, reader identity, and preservice teacher identity development. She is the co-author of *Two Years in the Life of Two English Teachers: To Be, To Do, To Become, Using Young Adult Literature to Work through Wobble Moments in Teacher Education: Literary Response Groups to Enhance Reflection and Understanding,* and *Novice Teachers Embracing Wobble in Standardized Schools: Using Dialogue and Inquiry for Self-Reflection and Growth.* Her work can also be found in *English Journal, ALAN Review* and *Voices from the Middle.*

Acknowledgments

This book about dialogic approaches to reading and literature is the product of many dialogues with some of my favorite people.

I am grateful for my editor Megha Patel and her editorial assistant Shivranjani Singh from Routledge for their collective expertise, direction, and insight which shaped this final product, as well as for my copy editor Nick Brock for his close reading and attention to detail. I owe a huge thank you to my colleagues Debbie Dean, Karen Brown, and Jon Ostenson for the reading and re-reading of drafts and sharing feedback. Thanks also to Bob Fecho for introducing me to dialogical theories, participating in countless dialogues, and ongoing mentoring. I also owe a huge debt of gratitude to my graduate assistants Mercedes Allen and Kaylee Smedley for their tireless, meticulous editing and attention to detail as they reviewed each chapter, as well as to Kaylee Smedley and Skyler Coombs for creating many of the images. Many thanks also to the Brigham Young University College of Humanities for sponsoring my summer at the National Humanities Center, which helped make this project possible. Tremendous thanks go to my running partners, dear friends, and family who participated in countless dialogues that kept me going as I worked on this project, as well as for keeping me healthy, fed, and entertained. And most especially thank you to the teachers whose wonderful work is highlighted in these pages: Jeanie Christensen, JC Leishman, Marion Morrow, Kaylee Smedley, Mercedes Allen, Abby Scoresby, Kara Trammell, Matti Hingano, Madison Simpson, and Abby Marchant.

And, finally, to those partners in dialogue who have supported me since my earliest days and continue to teach me through their experiences: My brothers and friends, Hayden, Skyler, and Terrance; their wives, Summer, Kellie, and Andrea; my nieces and nephews Ezra, Luke, Avery, Reagan, Reese, Grayson, Finley, and Brielle; and most especially my parents, Wendell and Venda, who champion whatever paths I pursue.

Foreword

Bob Fecho

My students more than once have heard me state that there is nothing more practical than theory. Oxymoronic though this may sound, it is a foundational, if you will, theory of mine. Although I stop short of writing that theory is a singular human trait—advances in science keep shooting down such distinctions—I do argue that all humans are theorizers, that we make sense of and operate in the world by conceiving, testing, and enacting theory. We see water damage on a ceiling and theorize where the leak might be. Someone you're seeing always has an excuse for not meeting your family and you cast about for reasons for the reluctance. The 5:03 train is always late on Fridays; while waiting for it, you shuffle through a few possibilities that might explain this trend. In other words, one doesn't have to be an Albert Einstein or a Hannah Arendt to truck in theory; one simply has to be human. *Theoriam creo, ergo sum.*

What makes theory practical is our willingness to live our theory, that is, to view the world through, make decisions based on, raise questions about, and reconsider our theories. A theory is not irrefutable fact. It is a postulate, a place marker, a possibility—all open to further exploration and reflection as contexts, which are always in flux, shift. As close as we might hold a theory to our core, we need to be ever willing to review, expand, refine, question, or even jettison it if new evidence comes to light. Discovering the limitations of our theories is as useful as delving into the opportunities and understandings they present.

Caring and insightful teachers are theorizers about teaching and learning. Dawan Coombs, the author of this book, is a caring and insightful teacher. Therefore, Dawan theorizes about teaching and learning. In particular, Dawan wonders about the ways dialogue creates a learning space that encourages all attending within to share their experiences and beliefs, to listen to and understand through the experiences and beliefs of others, and to individually and collectively construct meaning from that mutual engagement. She seeks generative dialogue (Hermans & Hermans-Konopka, 2010), shared utterances that go beyond ruminative response and, instead, create opportunities for self and others to transact "in the service of a further development of self and society" (p. 174). Her theory and her practice remain in continuous dialogue.

In this book, Dawan explores why and how to enter into dialogue with text, specifically to read and engage with what transactional theorist Louise Rosenblatt (1983) has deemed to be "merely inkspots on paper" until transformed into meaning by a reader. "What," Dawan ponders, "does it mean for readers—challenged, proficient, avid, aliterate, and what have you—to view reading not as a mechanical chore, but as opportunity to enter into a willing exchange of ideas and experiences?" Such a stance values neither author nor reader over the other, but celebrates the generative dialogue constructed between the two that results in an unfinalizable construction of meaning.

Reading, when considered through a dialogical stance, interrupts the atomization of an English Language Arts (ELA) curriculum. Rather than seeing each assigned or self-selected text as a one off (*Beloved* was yesterday. On to *Macbeth*), teachers and students alike begin to grasp the interconnectedness of their experiences and the texts they are re-creating (What drives Sethe in *Beloved* and Macbeth to commit crimes that haunt them?). As such, the dialogue is not just engagement with the text of the present, but with all past texts and those yet to come. Additionally, reading dialogically positions a reader to mindfully bring their prior experiences and understandings to the text, to experience that text, and then to consider what that exchange means for future experiences and understandings.

As suggested above, Dawan lives her theory. How she has taught reading as a secondary teacher and how she currently instructs aspiring secondary teachers are manifestations of her dialogical stance on education. The intersection of those practices are evident throughout this book. From an opening chapter that lays the groundwork for her discussion of the need to see reading as dialogical, she segues into the middle chapters that systematically and surehandedly provide both rationales and practical approaches toward integrating dialogue. But these chapters don't depict step-by-step, follow-the-numbers activities destined for rote replication. Instead, Dawan provides frameworks that invite readers to dialogue with the activities she shares as examples. Her intention is to inspire teachers to build outward from these frameworks and develop a dialogical stance on reading grounded in their classroom contexts and practices. Importantly, she concludes the book with a reminder of the significance of such work, of cautions to observe, and of possibilities to explore.

As I'm writing this foreword, events domestically and internationally are drawing attention to a world bereft of dialogue. National and world leaders too often talk in simplistic absolutes rather than acknowledge the complexity of issues. Reports in the media illustrate reading and viewing trends indicating that consumers of news tend to access only one aspect of an issue, that being the one with which they already agree. Rather than dialogue that might expand or nuance understanding, many citizens in the US and the world prefer confirmation and, ultimately, reification of beliefs.

What Dawan provides in this book is an attempt to ready the citizens of coming generations for raising questions about, seeking multiple understandings of, and taking critical dialogical stances on whatever texts they choose to encounter or have thrust on them. She doesn't assume that a dialogical approach to reading is innate. Rather, she asserts through argument and example that such an approach to reading is eminently teachable, as well as of complete necessity. Fittingly, Dawan reflects a thought espoused by a Middle East peace activist profiled in Colum McCann's (2020) *Apeirogon*. Referring to the complex issues facing Palestinians and Israelis, he points to a sticker on his motorbike: "This won't be over until we talk." What polarization exists in the worlds we create will only be ended through dialogue. Dawan suggests we do that one reader and one reading at a time.

References

Hermans, H. & Hermans-Konopka, A. (2010). *Dialogical self theory: Positioning and counter-positioning in a globalizing society*. Cambridge University Press.
McCann, C. (2020). *Apeirogon*. Random House.
Rosenblatt, L. (1983). *Literature as exploration*. MLA.

1

Exploring a Dialogical Approach to Teaching Literature

One of my favorite fictional teachers in young adult literature is Lieutenant Colonel Hupfer from Gary Schmidt's 2023 *The Labors of Hercules Beal*—although initially it might be hard to see why. On his first day of 7th grade at the Cape Cod Academy for Environmental Sciences, Hercules encounters Lieutenant Colonel Hupfer—an ex-Marine spending the rest of his civilian years teaching English. The Lieutenant seems to have it in for Hercules and his peers, running his class more like bootcamp than book club. The guy exhibits the warmth of an ice cube and when one student mouths off or steps out of line, all of them pay. So, a few weeks into the school year when the Lieutenant rolls out "a yearlong mission" for the class, the students assume it's a unique form of torture that only an ex-Marine could concoct.

This mission turns out to be anything but a typical investigation into classical mythology. Instead of reading myths and writing reports, Lieutenant Colonel Hupfer issues orders that tap into students' unique cultures, interests, and strengths to help them make personally relevant connections to their study of the mythology (as well as regular 500-word reflections reporting their progress). For Alyssa de la Peña, it meant creating 144 maps charting the journeys of the major gods and goddesses (after she figured out where those journeys had taken them). For Malcolm, the class doodler, it meant creating a graphic novel of

The Odyssey (but he had to read it first). And for Hercules Beal, who was named after the mythic Hercules himself, it meant attempting the monumental task of completing his own version of the Twelve Labors of Hercules in his small coastal New England town.

As far as pedagogy goes, I admired Lieutenant Colonel Hupfer's approach. The projects, as he explained, came individually customized for each student, designed to help them learn both about classical myths and themselves through reading, action, and reflection—all staples of any quality English language arts curriculum. Most of the missions involved a year's worth of study and reading about elements of mythology and culture as well as forging connections between the content of the reading and the lives of the students. And, of course, their work included reflection, reflection, and reflection. Although fictional, these assignments seemed relevant, engaging, and helped students understand literature and their own lives better because of their studies.

Maybe I also appreciated these assignments because, as a high school teacher, I remember constantly searching for ways to help students see connections between their own lives and the literature we read. I wanted to help students create a dialogue between the literature and their lives. It wasn't that my students couldn't read, but motivating them to open a book, to dive deeply into its content, and to explore the relevance of the ideas in their own lives proved challenging. They constantly asked me "What's the point of this?" Although I wanted them to read, comprehend, and analyze texts, I knew they needed motivation to explore how the texts spoke to their questions about the world, the challenges they faced, and their interests. I craved strategies that would help my students forge connections to texts and actively engage with ideas.

To their credit, most of my students would try anything that provided a break from what they perceived as traditional reading and writing practices. The skeptics in the class wondered at the legitimacy of anything that seemed to bear the slightest semblance of "fun," but if the teacher sanctioned it, they figured it was okay. A few others questioned anything that didn't seem to reflect the "rigor" of lectures and note taking they sometimes experienced in classes, but we all experimented together.

I tried integrating artifacts like horseshoes and red dresses into the study of *Of Mice and Men*, which added tangible elements into explorations of symbols and meaning within the text. I cautiously attempted simulating small-scale discrimination based on favorite college basketball teams, which eventually launched powerful discussions about real-life discrimination and injustice in my 10th grade classes when we studied *To Kill a Mockingbird*. With the help of a creative colleague, we invited our juniors to critically examine environmental print and advertisements to interrogate the commercialization of culture while reading *Tuesdays With Morrie*. These activities seemed to increase students' willingness to engage in the inquiry and see how the readings in class pertained to their lives. In much smaller ways these activities achieved a similar purpose to Lieutenant Colonel Hupfer's mythology project—they stimulated interest in reading by drawing connections and creating dialogue between the texts of students' lives, the texts we read, and their worlds.

But at the time I wasn't entirely sure why these strategies worked, how I might justify them to skeptical parents or administrators, or how to replicate their success. Now, with hindsight that comes from time and a better understanding of theory and research, I realize that these types of learning experiences fit within the framework of dialogical pedagogy—what Bob Fecho (2011) defined as approaches to teaching and learning that promote dialogue between students, dialogue with the teacher, dialogue with texts, and dialogue with the contexts of students' lives.

These kinds of dialogues align with what fourth volume of the *Handbook of Reading Research* described as the "dialogic turn" in reading comprehension. In contrast to approaches that emphasize the teaching of reading strategies in isolation, dialogic approaches rely on teaching reading in context—particularly through content-rich instruction, discussion and dialogue between students and teachers, argumentation that explores multiple perspectives, and the use of a variety of texts to support student comprehension (Wilkinson & Son, 2011).

In their own ways each of these practices puts readers in the midst of the dialogues Bob advocates for—those with classmates and teachers, with texts, and with the context of the world to support comprehension.

Although numerous studies reflect the value of each of these elements in reading comprehension for elementary readers, less is known about what happens when dialogic approaches are used to support adolescent readers. And yet, recent findings from educational psychology research on reading motivation, neuroscience research on the reading brain, and educational research on reading comprehension offer new insights from across fields that provide increased support for integrating these approaches into reading and literature instruction to help secondary students read and comprehend texts. In addition, the dialogic nature of these strategies and the need for students now—perhaps more than ever—to dialogue across differences adds increased reasons for including these approaches in secondary classrooms.

But what might it mean to take a dialogical approach to teaching reading and literature in the secondary classroom? How would dialogical approaches help students find relevance and interest in texts and support reading comprehension? How might teachers craft dialogical strategies that help readers engage with texts? These questions about the application of theory to practice led me to invite a handful of secondary English, language arts, and reading teachers to see how integrating dialogic approaches and strategies in their own classrooms supported reading comprehension.

This book shares what we found, both in terms of a framework for conceptualizing and enacting dialogic approaches as well as practical strategies for engaging students in the study of literary and informational texts. This first chapter explores the concept of dialogism and how it has informed the teaching of English and language arts, including the research on the teaching of reading across the grades. It then illustrates how reading itself is a dialogical process. The last part of the chapter describes how content-rich instruction, discussion, argumentation, and intertextuality provide a framework for strategies and approaches for the teaching reading and literature at the secondary level that engage students in the study of texts, create connections between their lives and literature, and increase their comprehension.

What Do You Mean by "Dialogic"?

Before we get much further into this pedagogical adventure, we should unpack the term "dialogic" together. Dialogic perspectives resonate with many researchers and practitioners across the field of education today, resulting in an abundance of research and resources that promote dialogic approaches to teaching and learning generally. Just search the phrase "dialogic teaching" and you'll find almost five million results online. But what does it mean to be dialogic and why does a dialogic approach matter when teaching reading and literature in today's classrooms?

"Dialogic" literally means characterized by dialogue or conversation with another. At the root of most dialogic approaches are principles from the theories of Mikhail Bakhtin, Lev Vygotsky, Paulo Freire, and other thinkers who emphasized the importance of learning and developing through dialogue. Although their individual theories vary slightly, each of these thinkers saw dialogue with others, with texts, and with the world as the catalyst for engaged, meaning-filled, authentic inquiry. In practice, these theories mean that teachers serve as facilitators of learning rather than conveyors of information and together students and teachers wrestle with questions and construct meaning. As learners question and consider the perspectives of others, inquiry leads them to answers and more questions in a process of learning that doesn't really have an end.

Right now you might be thinking "Yes, but what do these ideas mean in terms of what I do in my classroom?" because—at least on the surface—the previous paragraph sounds like a lot of theory and not a lot of practical application. But amidst the hundreds of strategies and practices you might choose to use tomorrow in class, your beliefs about learning dictate which strategies, practices, and approaches you'll ultimately use. So, think for a minute about what you value in teaching and then see if any of the practices that follow resonate with your beliefs.

Dialogical beliefs are almost inherent in the curriculum of English and language arts. They value talk, language, and learners in meaning making. At the heart of dialogical teaching is the idea that people learn best through dialogue with other people and the world. A teacher might lecture about the meaning of a poem or a story, but students typically learn best (and engage more) when they discuss the work with others. One implication of a dialogical approach means opting for teaching strategies that invite students to talk in small groups with their peers to create meaning or to discuss the work with the class.

Researchers like Martin Nystrand and Mary Juzwik, whose work examines how to facilitate dialogic classroom talk, encourage teachers to use strategies such as Socratic seminars, fishbowl discussions, and literature circles to integrate meaningful conversations about literature, language, and ideas in their classrooms. These practices are embedded with structures that help students focus on tasks and allow them to co-construct meaning together. The social nature of these approaches, and the autonomy they offer students, align not only with dialogical theory but also with research on motivation and engagement.

Dialogic beliefs can also inform how teachers approach the teaching of writing. A dialogical approach to writing would use writing as a way for students to participate in authentic dialogue with others and the world around them. The work of practitioner-focused researchers like Bob Fecho explores dialogical approaches to teaching writing that incorporate students' lives, cultures, and experiences into the writing curriculum of the English language arts (ELA) classroom. In these writing assignments students interview people in their worlds, write in genres that they value—such as comics, music, or videos—and even offer critiques of institutions or traditions in the form of public service announcements, speeches, and community action projects. In fostering dialogues with the world around them, these writing opportunities also capitalize on principles of motivation as they integrate relevance and interest to make these products connected to students' lives.

As a former ELA teacher, I appreciate the way these strategies and approaches exemplify principles of dialogue and the way they inform how I think about teaching writing, literature, speaking, and listening. They center the student in the learning and consider ways to bring relevance, purpose, and community into teaching and learning. As a researcher and a teacher of reading and literature, I am most passionate about how dialogical theories can expand the way secondary teachers think about teaching reading and the possibilities these approaches hold for supporting the adolescents in our classes.

Earlier in the chapter I mentioned the "dialogic turn" taking place in reading comprehension. Unlike past approaches that emphasized teaching strategies in isolation, dialogical approaches to teaching reading emphasize the relationship between context, dialogue, and comprehension. Specifically, through content-rich instruction, discussion, argumentation, and intertextual approaches, teachers and students work together to make meaning from texts and support comprehension (Wilkinson & Son, 2011). Like the approaches to writing, speaking, and listening, these dialogical elements require readers to dialogue with classmates and teachers, with texts, and with the context of the world as a part of the process of making sense of the literature they read.

But what do these principles mean for teachers' practice? Typically, context-rich instruction looks like the integration of strategies within the teaching of rich, subject-matter content that centers inquiry and collaboration in the learning process. Teachers model strategies, then students practice applying strategies as they read texts for authentic inquiry purposes that also build content knowledge. This most often takes place in science and social studies through practices like Concept-Oriented Reading Instruction (CORI) (Guthrie et al., 2004) and Reading Apprenticeship (Schoenbach et al., 2003) that help students make real-world connections and become subject experts through inquiry and meaningful reading.

Discussion values engaging different perspectives or points of view, sharing reactions to and reflections on the text, and learning from peers through both formalized discussion protocols and informal discussions. Practices like book clubs (Raphael & McMahon, 1994), literature circles (Daniels, 2004), Questioning the Author (Beck & McKeown, 2006), and reciprocal teaching (Palincsar & Brown, 1984) represent just a few applications of discussion-centered pedagogy (see Table 1.1).

TABLE 1.1 Dialogical strategies

Dialogic strategy	Description
Book clubs (Raphael & McMahon, 1994)	Organize students in small groups (usually four or five) according to their interest in a particular text, the readability of the text, and students' ability to work together. Because the groups are reading different texts, students set their own reading schedules and complete the readings on their own. As they read, students note discussion points they want to raise with their peers and when the book club meets, students direct the focus of their dialogues. Students co-construct meaning and wrestle with interpretations together.
Literature circles (Daniels, 2004)	Like book clubs, students are organized into groups of four or five and each group reads a book selected based on student interest, readability, and group dynamics. Students read together or on their own, but the discussion is more structured than in book clubs because each student assumes responsibility to fulfill a role. Typically, roles include discussion director, wordsmith, questioner, summarizer, and visualizer, but teachers often integrate other roles as well. These roles help students work through the text and make meaning together.
Questioning the author (QtA) (Beck & McKeown, 2006)	Students work independently, in pairs, in small groups or with the whole class to ask questions of a text's author. Instead of assuming the text contains all the necessary information presented in a clear manner, QtA helps students see texts as the thoughts of the author who can be questioned or who might leave out information. Therefore, after reading, the teacher and students ask and answer questions about what the author is trying to say, why the author says it, whether it is clear, and how the author could have been clearer. Students discuss their answers to the questions, then collaborate as they revise their answers.
Reciprocal teaching (Palincsar & Brown, 1984)	Reciprocal teaching helps students work together to read and comprehend texts. Students take turns reading and directing the group's progress through the text while each member of the group assumes responsibility for a different strategy—summarizing, making predictions, clarifying, and asking questions. Focusing on these strategies helps initiate student talk as they work together to comprehend the text.

(Continued)

TABLE 1.1 (Continued)

Dialogic strategy	Description
Jigsaw (Aronson, 2002)	Students first meet in their home groups (usually 4–6 students) to review the reading task and then to identify their expert group assignments. Then, they move to their corresponding expert groups to read and discuss content with other students in the class who are also charged with becoming experts on the material. In the final stage, students return to their home groups and teach one another what they learned in their expert groups. Each takes a turn as the "expert" and shares their understandings with the group.
Socratic seminars (Elfie, 2002)	A student-centered discussion facilitated by the teacher but driven by students' questions. These typically take place around a text or shared inquiry and involve the sharing of evidence, critical reasoning, and whole-group dialogue in response to one another.
Fishbowl discussions (Baloche et al., 1993)	Students are organized in an inner and outer circle and participate differently in each space. The inner circle students discuss a topic or inquiry question in a similar manner to those in a Socratic Seminar, asking questions, sharing evidence, and engaging in critical reasoning. At the same time, the students in the outer circle take notes. Then the roles switch and the students in the inner circle move to the outer circle and those formerly in the outer circle engage in the conversation, drawing on their notes and insights to continue the dialogue.
Question–answer relationship (QAR) (Fordham, 2006)	This strategy helps students understand how to ask better questions by teaching them the different types of questions that help readers understand texts. Students read a section of a text and ask different types of questions, including "right there" questions where the answer exists directly in the text, "think and search" questions that require synthesizing and making inferences, "author and you" questions that require readers to connect their own experiences to ideas in the text, and "on my own" questions that demand readers construct their answers based on their background knowledge. This strategy can be used independently, in small groups, or as a whole class to help students ask better questions that lead to fruitful discussions as well as how to use the text to find answers.

(*Continued*)

TABLE 1.1 (Continued)

Dialogic strategy	Description
Concept-oriented reading instruction (Guthrie et al., 2004)	CORI integrates science and reading to engage students in hands-on learning that supports reading comprehension of informational texts. Teachers help activate students' background knowledge to ignite their excitement about learning; then students participate in questioning, reading, summarizing, and discussions about texts.
Collaborative reasoning (Clark et al., 2003; Zhang & Stahl, 2011)	Students are organized into small groups and work together to read and analyze a text. Instead of the teacher leading the discussion, students identify their beliefs and understandings, gathering evidence from their experiences and their readings to support their positions. Then students present their arguments and rationales, and their peers question their arguments and sources. Sharing and asking questions helps stimulate critical thinking and personal engagement as they co-construct meaning.
Reading apprenticeship (Schoenbach et al., 2003)	This framework helps students collaborate with peers to work through reading challenges. They begin by reading a text, then responding to a question about what they believe using evidence from the text and their own experiences to support their beliefs; then they share their beliefs with one another, listening respectfully and asking questions to clarify. These discussions take place within co-created guidelines and are peer-led.

In the early grades dialogic book reading also offers ways to bring children and adults into conversation with one another about texts as they engage in making predictions, discussing open-ended questions, describing characters and events, and making connections between the ideas in the book and the readers' own lives (Arnold et al., 1994). Similarly, argumentation draws on student perspectives and understandings to share evidence to support claims, explore perspectives, and examine multiple viewpoints using practices such as collaborative reasoning (Clark et al., 2003) and the use of claim, evidence, and reasoning.

Finally, intertextuality considers the role other texts—including written texts, hands-on experiences that help students make sense of texts, and generalizations shared by students or teachers—play in helping scaffold and support comprehension. Practices such as the pairing of informational and fiction texts or two nonfiction texts on the same topic (Camp, 2000) or interactive read alouds (Fisher et al., 2011) encourage teachers and students to work together to make meaning. Intertextuality also includes experiments, experiential learning, and other hands-on tasks.

Although numerous studies describe the value of different dialogical reading comprehension practices and strategies used with elementary students, far fewer reflect what happens when dialogic approaches are used to support adolescent readers. In particular, a number of intertextual approaches central to creating dialogic reading experiences are often underutilized in secondary classrooms beyond science and history. And yet, considering the research that suggests adolescents (even more than elementary students) value collaboration and need motivational supports, dialogic approaches seem ideally suited for them. Exploring these possibilities in the contexts of the teaching of reading and literature in secondary classrooms is the purpose of this book. But before we get there, first we need to talk about what it means to read and how the act of reading is, in and of itself, a dialogue between the reader and the text.

How Is Reading a Dialogic Experience?

This dialogic turn resonates with theories put forth by theorists like Mikhail Bakhtin, Paulo Freire, and Louise Rosenblatt who, close to 100 years ago, used the concept of dialogue to describe what takes place in the mind of the reader as they make sense of texts. Although at the time these theorists didn't have the neuroscience research to back up their theories, their descriptions of the reading process sound remarkably similar to what modern-day cognitive neuroscientists describe as happening in the brain as readers makes sense of sounds, symbols, memories, and feelings and how all of these contribute to our ability to comprehend texts.

Let's begin with a word. Freire (1983) explained that, on the most basic level, reading words required first "reading the world" because words only take on meaning in relation to our individual experiences and knowledge of the world in which we live (p. 11). Before we even know that letters represent sounds and different combinations of letters represent words, the words we speak have meaning—both common meanings shared with others and those unique to our own experiences with words. For example, you and I understand that the combination of the letters D-O-G refers to a furry four-legged canine often known for its loyalty to humans and steady companionship. But my individual experiences with Rocky and Wojo, the family dogs of my own child, teenage, and young adult years, probably differ from the image called up in your mind when you hear the combination of letters D-O-G and think of your own family pets (or lack thereof).

In addition, because I was a teenager in the late 1990s, when I hear D-O-G spoken aloud I also think of the countless times I watched *Finding Forrester* (2000), hearing Jamal Wallace and his friends refer to one another as "dog" and Sean Connery's character exclaim "You're the man now, dog!" with an Irish brogue. I even think about my younger brother Hayden, who my father affectionately nicknamed "Haydsdog," a mashup between his name and the second syllable of "corndog," which is what the two used to eat for lunch together on a far too regular basis. The term D-O-G also calls up faint memories of times I may have occasionally been "dogged" or let down by people in my social group—and then there are the images of the rapper Snoop Dogg cheering on the USA at the Paris Olympics. And, most especially, when I hear the word D-O-G, I cannot not see the mascot of my alma mater and favorite college football team, the Georgia Bulldogs, nor can I stop myself from yelling "Go Dawgs!"

Depending on the degree of overlap between our experiences, we may or may not share some of these associations between the word and the world. Members of my family will share the connection between the word and our pet dogs, but for you the term D-O-G may bring to your mind images and names of breeds of dogs that I don't even realize exist. Regardless of your affinity for dogs, you likely have many associations with this word beyond those that I've shared (which, like it or not, are now a part of your associations with this term too). Still other variations exist beyond our individual or collective worlds. You too might be shouting "Go Dawgs," but those words mean something entirely different when shouted by Washington Huskies fans as opposed to Georgia Bulldogs fans. These are just a handful of examples that show how a single word embodies an individual's experiences, beliefs, feelings, and understandings, but all of these are called up in our brains when we hear the combination of letters D-O-G, that we then sort through to select the likely most accurate or appropriate meaning to associate with the word we read.

Although the overlaps and connections I described here have long been the stuff of theory, research in neuroscience confirms the role reading the world plays in reading words. In more technical terms, neuroscientist and reading expert Maryanne Wolf (2018) described how neurons create actual live circuits in our brains that link letters to sounds, then string sounds together to make a word. Once the word is formed, other areas of the brain draw on short and long-term memory to link the word to memories to a breadth and depth of meanings from which the brain identifies the meaning of the word.

This linking takes place in the form of nerve impulses that occur in moments imperceptible to the reader. Maryanne Wolf (2016) explained that it's during the first 300–500 milliseconds of reading that we as readers "connect what our world teaches us about the *word*…with *what* we have learned as a 'totality' of knowledge from the *world* immediately following it" (p. 110). In this small space of time "each word can elicit an entire history of myriad connections, associations, and long-storied emotions" that "momentarily activate whole repositories of associated meanings, memories, and feelings, even when the exact meaning in a given context is specified" (Wolf, 2018, p. 33). That is, during this space of time almost too quick to measure, the reading brain combines and assimilates knowledge of how words work, how symbols function, which sounds they represent, and what those words mean with the reader's knowledge of the world, created through their own experiences, their personal backgrounds, and the moments they've experienced vicariously through reading and from the stories of others.

All of this happens in the mind of each reader with *each word*. Now scale that to the sentence, paragraph, and book level. The words combine to form sentences, the sentences cumulate into paragraphs, the paragraphs comprise chapters, and the chapters a book. The details of this process vary depending on the purpose for reading in the reader's mind and the type of the text, but the processes are roughly the same. Think about all the neurons firing and the work happening in your brain in order to comprehend and make meaning as your eyes fly across a text! It's for this reason that so many theorists and researchers alike describe reading as an active and dynamic process that takes place as readers make sense of texts.

Rosenblatt (2005) explained this process that takes place between reader and text as a "transaction," where meaning doesn't come "ready-made 'in' the text or 'in' the reader," but occurs when readers interpret the text through the lens of their own experiences, beliefs, feelings, understandings, and customs, bringing words to life (p. 7). When the reader and the text transact, it creates a "live circuit" that links meaning to the words on the page. In these transactions, meaning exists neither in the text nor in the head of the reader; rather, meaning is created as the reader "brings to the work personality traits, memories of past events, present needs and preoccupations, a particular mood of the moment, and a particular physical condition" to make sense of the text on the page in the unique context of the reading experience (p. 30). In other words, the transaction is the path through which the meaning is created between the reader and the text.

In both theory and science, Wolf, Rosenblatt, Freire, and Bakhtin (plus many others) recognized that—whether reading a single word (like in our D-O-G example), or reading a whole book—individual experiences, feelings, understandings, and knowledge shape the meanings readers give to words. The role of dialogue matters in these approaches to reading and literature because reading and understanding cannot be separated from the contexts of the reader's life, experiences, feelings, and understandings. The words on a page or in a book or on a screen are in dialogue with the world of the reader. As readers read words and link them to ideas, words take on meaning within the larger frameworks and ways readers make sense of the world. Because every reader constantly experiences new events, encounters, understandings, people, and places over time and in different contexts, and because most continue to read, no reader is ever the same from one day to the next. As a result, a word, a passage, or a whole text each contains an individualized meaning, unique to the reader in a specific time and place of the reader's experience.

When literature resonates with students' lives or with concepts they want to better understand, it evokes an emotional reaction and personalizes the reading experience. Maryanne Wolf (2016) described these kinds of connections as powerful contributors to the creation of the reading circuit as the brain builds "expanding, interactive sets of relationships among our background knowledge, the contents of our reading, and our insights into them both" (p. 122). In other words, to comprehend texts readers need to dialogue with their past experiences and texts. Research shows that reading—more than movies or TV or other forms of story consumption—allows readers to feel as if they are the character in the story (Berns, 2002). In these ways reading invites students into a laboratory that simulates what it's like to be another person, including their emotions and challenges (Wolf, 2018).

Expressed more succinctly, these dialogues form connections and these connections matter—not just for surface-level meaning-making or comprehension, but because they are foundational components of deep reading. As Maryanne Wolf (2018) explained,

> Deep reading is always about *connection*: connecting what we know to what we read, what we read to what we feel, what we feel to what we think, and how we think to how we live out our lives in a connected world.
>
> (p. 163)

In other words, sounding out words is not enough to evoke deep reading. In addition to decoding words, adolescents need to situate what they read within the context of what they already know to comprehend what they read and build on their understandings. They need to be dialoguing with texts in ways that link the world of the book with their own lives, emotions, questions, and ideas.

Amid our current social, political, and cultural divisions, perspective taking may potentially be one of the biggest benefits of reading—to see and empathize with the other. But often those connections, emotions, and dialogues don't happen spontaneously in the minds and hearts of readers. For students who don't have feelings for books and cannot connect with texts, implementing dialogical strategies offers opportunities to help students make sense of texts and see through the lens of the other and engage in the reading experience.

Crafting Dialogical Opportunities of Adolescent Readers

As I think about all that happens in the minds of readers as they link sounds, symbols, and meaning to their feelings, past experiences, and knowledge, I think about Travis, a 9th grader from rural Georgia that I met a few years ago. He sat in the back of the room and didn't say much in class, but he agreed to talk with me about his reading habits. As I got to know him, I learned that he lived with his mom and dad, his uncle fought in the Vietnam War, and—even though Travis didn't like reading—he loved stories that helped him understand his uncle's wartime experiences. He described himself as "just not a sit-down person," but as a "hands-on person," as someone who liked sports and doing things better than just sitting around. His mom was a reader, he saw value in reading, and he knew reading made kids in his class smarter, but he also just couldn't get into it. He explained:

> I don't really have emotions for books. I just don't get 'em...When my teacher made me start reading, I tried to read it. I mean, I can read 'em, but I just don't have emotions for them. They're just words.

I empathized with his challenge, but at the time I didn't realize the power of his description. However, the more I understand the theory and research that explains what happens in our brains when we read, the more I realize Travis couldn't have more articulately described the challenge with reading that he and so many other adolescents face. Although he had the ability to sound out words, the links between words, meaning, and emotion seemed absent. For Travis and countless other adolescents like him, sounding out words was not the issue; it was the linking of meaning and feeling between the words, phrases, sentences, and paragraphs that proved problematic.

As "not a sit-down person" and a more "hands-on person," Travis wanted to do something active, something that helped him feel emotion and engaged his interests. It's not that Travis didn't have a wealth of personal experiences, interests, feelings, and knowledge relevant to the texts his teachers wanted him to read—he brought plenty to the reading experience. But, like many adolescents, "with no discernable link to the perceived world around them, [they] find that long, abstract texts are not only meaningless, but are also aversive and painful to cope with" (Douglass & Guthrie, 2008, p. 22). He had his knowledge, skills, experiences, and interests relevant to the text, but he couldn't—or didn't know how—to make these connections on his own while reading. He couldn't "do" it.

Travis and an increasing number of students in this post-pandemic era of teaching struggle with reading and engagement. The teaching of reading and literature—particularly in secondary schools—is fraught with complexity because adolescent reading difficulties stem from a variety of issues. Some struggle with undiagnosed learning disabilities or challenges that come with neurodiversity; others haven't developed the decoding, fluency, and vocabulary skills necessary to perform reading tasks. Others struggle because of motivational issues, and still others from disconnects between their home cultures and the culture of school. It's not that these students lack the potential to develop reading abilities. However, they often do not see relevance in the reading they are assigned, or the texts do not appeal to their interests.

Students' individual interests offer natural entry points into books because through these interests reading becomes relevant and intrinsically motivating (Fink, 1995). Beyond textbooks and canonical texts, engaging trade books, quality YA fiction and nonfiction, and contemporary fiction represent a variety of cultures and experiences that offer meaningful reading experiences that reflect the conflicts, themes, and dilemmas of students' lives. As teachers design their curriculum around student interests, teachers provide motivation and support that facilitates reading growth (McRae & Guthrie, 2009) and autonomy for students to make decisions about their own learning (Troyer, 2017). And, when students study topics of interest to them, they work harder and learn more (Hagay et al., 2012). Interest-based approaches help students who otherwise see themselves as nonreaders engage with texts in meaningful ways (Ivey & Johnston, 2023, Rodesiler et al., 2024).

But any teacher knows that teaching only to students' interests proves challenging because of the myriad of different interests even within one class, and also because the standards dictate which skills students need to develop and schoolwide and district curriculum often determine which texts will be used in the teaching. No matter how well-intentioned, sometimes students don't get to choose what they read, particularly in content area classes where specific topics must be addressed.

In these instances, for students like Travis that crave active engagement and who need help feeling emotions for books, teachers need to intentionally craft opportunities to make connections, to identify and access emotions, and to dialogue with the text and then scaffold them into the reading experience. For these students, dialogical approaches to reading and literature may hold the key to helping secondary teachers conceptualize reading experiences that support comprehension and engagement.

The Possibilities of Dialogical Reading in Secondary Classrooms

At the beginning of this chapter, I described the dialogical turn in reading instruction, which values content-rich instruction, discussion, argumentation, and intertextual approaches to help teachers and students make meaning from texts and support comprehension. These approaches, although prevalent in an increasing number of elementary classrooms, are less commonly adopted and practiced in secondary classrooms. However, when applied to the study of reading and literature at the secondary level, they offer powerful tools for creating engaged reading experiences for students like Travis.

Travis wanted reading to "do" something—to be active, to help him pursue his interests, and to accomplish something he cared about. I believe dialogical approaches to teaching reading and literature can capitalize on the desire to "do" by harnessing intertextual strategies that put students in active dialogue with the themes, conflicts, characters, and ideas in texts, in their lives, and with others. In the final section of this chapter, I sketch out an approach to reading and literature instruction that engages students in deep reading through applications of these principles:

- ♦ Content-rich instruction that draws on the contexts of students' lives, experiences, and interests to initiate inquiry and authentic dialogue.
- ♦ Intertextual strategies that help students make meaning of texts through other texts and experiences.
- ♦ Discussions where students and teachers co-construct knowledge about texts and ideas that thrive on questions and response.
- ♦ Argumentation that values using evidence to support multiple perspectives and interpretations.

Practices informed by these dialogical principles can help teachers facilitate content-rich instruction that utilizes intertextual experiences to help students "do" reading and dialogue with texts, with one another, and with the world.

Content-Rich Instruction that Draws on the Contexts of Students' Lives, Experiences, and Interests to Initiate Authentic Inquiry and Dialogue

Content-rich instruction integrates the teaching of strategies and the meaningful study of substantive disciplinary content. In a dialogical framework rich content includes not just important discipline-specific knowledge, but authentic, student-driven inquiries built on students' goals for learning and connecting the content with the contexts of their lives. The examples throughout this book illustrate how the texts, concepts, and skills at the heart of content-rich inquiries invite students to dialogue with the conflicts, characters, and themes in literature.

Students need to master disciplinary-specific content as well as the strategies described in the standards. But a wide range of high-quality and high-interest texts can be used to teach standards for reading and analyzing literary and nonfiction. Content-rich instruction integrates the contexts of students' lives with the curriculum through texts that respond to and reflect their cultures and interests. Considering a diversity of texts helps teachers create links between each student's "knowledge, social disposition, and competencies for information seeking" and the content they need to teach, thereby bridging building "motivational qualities of out-of-school literacy with the content of academic curriculum" (Guthrie et al., 2006, pp. 85–86).

Like culturally relevant education, content-rich instruction draws on students' rich and diverse backgrounds to make learning more relevant, meaningful, and effective, particularly those on the margins of the classrooms (Gay, 2010; Ladson-Billings, 1995). In the chapters that follow, the strategies and concepts are anchored in the reading of canonical texts and YA texts from a variety of genres and in different formats. But regardless of the strategy or text, the teacher situates the reading tasks within the context of students' lives, make explicit links to students' backgrounds, cultures, and interests and foster connections that make reading texts relevant, interesting, and engaging.

Intertextual Strategies that Help Students Discover Meaning in Texts Through Dialogues with Other Texts, Experiences, Classmates, and Teachers

In their discussion of features of dialogical instruction, Wilkinson and Son (2011) described intertextuality as "the sine qua non" (or essential condition) for dialogic reading experiences (p. 374). This is because other texts—be they written, oral, media, or hands-on experiences—provide alternative representations of ideas that can help mediate understanding, strengthen background knowledge, and situate ideas within contexts that motivate students to read and learn more.

For students like Travis, hands-on experiences generate relevance for and interest in reading. Motivation researchers use the term "stimulating tasks" to describe games, simulations, drama, puzzles, and manipulatives that create temporary interest in topics (Nolen & Nichols, 1994; Guthrie et al., 2006; Zahorik, 1996). The magic behind these active, learning-by-doing tasks lies in their ability to trigger situational interest—a state of short-term interest in a topic or task—that focuses students' attention, increases their knowledge, and creates a positive emotional tone towards the learning experience (Guthrie et al., 2006; Krapp et al., 1992; Schiefele, 2009). But to trigger situational interest, stimulating tasks need to be substantive, connected to the content, and followed by reading opportunities that allow students to continue to wrestle with the ideas and concepts (Nolen & Nichols, 1994). In other words, they need to be dialogic.

Under these conditions, stimulating tasks can be catalysts for engaged reading experiences. As Gibb and Guthrie (2008) explained,

> Real-world interactions, although a great source of experiential learning and fun, do not support engaged reading by themselves; they serve to arouse students' curiosity and as a launch pad to reading. When teachers supply an abundance of books on a topic to follow up on students' observations, we have seen deep student engagement in reading about that topic.
>
> (pp. 87–88)

They go on to describe findings from another study where an hour invested in generating interest through stimulating tasks led to 10 hours of engaged reading related to the task and topic (Guthrie et al., 2006). That's 10 hours of actual reading from students in exchange for one hour of hands-on activity invested during class. Think about that—what other strategies or activities yield that kind of return in deep reading that can develop into lasting, individual interest that sustains readers and motivates them to read independently (Hidi & Harackiewicz, 2000)?

In addition, incorporating hands-on components makes abstract concepts concrete and knowledge accessible through experience, regardless of students' mastery of the language. These strategies are particularly helpful for multilanguage learners and students who struggle with reading because hands-on activities offer a "touchable route for learning" that ignites curiosity that can be flamed with books (Taboada et al., 2008, p. 152). Similarly, hands-on experiences make language and literacy demands more accessible for students with disabilities and neurodiverse students (Dalton et al., 1997; Mastropieri et al., 1999). When supplemented with an abundance of texts and opportunities for reading deeply, these experiences provide a catalyst for content-rich inquiry. Stimulating tasks are the primary focus of the intertextual approaches illustrated throughout this book and the central focus of the illustrations that follow. These initiate connections with texts and create opportunities for dialogue among students.

Discussions Where Students and Teachers Co-construct Knowledge and that Thrive on Questions and Response

Both discussion and argument value—even center—social interactions around reading experiences where students learn from one another as they explore a diversity of perspectives. These interactions create a sense of relatedness and belonging that build student connection to one another and to texts as they interrogate authentic questions (Antonio & Guthrie, 2008). Content-rich studies initiated by engaging stimulating tasks can also foster equitable opportunities for all students to participate in the discussion and share a diversity of perspectives.

Dialogic approaches that are content-rich and that use stimulating tasks to cultivate curiosity provide catalysts for students to ask questions of texts and the world. In other words, they supplement meaningful inquiry. In a review of hands-on learning approaches, researchers discovered students who actively engaged in strategies that generated situational interest not only ask more questions, but also asked higher-quality questions about the topics and the readings (Ross, 1988). These authentic, student-generated questions are the very kind that students need to dialogue authentically with texts and with one another.

As students address their questions, dialogue takes place both through informal discussions and through formal questioning protocols that bring out all voices. Questioning is a powerful skill essential for good readers to develop, shaping not just their engagement with texts, but also what they take away from the reading experience (Duke & Pearson, 2002). A number of high-effect size strategies help students generate questions while they read, such as reciprocal teaching and QAR. These questions are relevant to students and reflect their engagement with ideas and issues relevant to their worlds. In this way content-rich inquiries initiated by stimulating tasks create a path to dialogic reading, questioning, and discussion among students.

Dialogical approaches also invite students to assume a critical stance, asking hard questions of themselves and their worlds (Appleman, 2023). Critical inquiries prove motivating for all students, but particularly for multilanguage learners and with students from diverse backgrounds (Aronson & Laughter, 2016). In these inquiries critical questions invite students to critique power structures and the world around them, adding an additional level of engagement and interest for students.

For students who struggle as readers, multilanguage learners, and neurodiverse students, simulating tasks also help them more actively participate in the co-construction of knowledge. As Guthrie et al. (2006) noted,

> Stimulating tasks are egalitarian. All students in the classroom can perform the stimulating task, connect it immediately to books, and experience situational interest for reading...Even for students with low initial interest in reading, participation in a stimulating task will foster reading interest, and the teacher can actively promote reading interest rather than wait for motivation to occur.
> (p. 244)

Part of the value of these dialogical approaches lies in the way they create a more equitable learning space where all students engage in the dialogue central to engaged reading experiences.

Argumentation that Values Using Evidence to Support Multiple Perspectives and Interpretations

One of my favorite quotes from Bakhtin (1984) ties together both the role of discussion and argument in dialogical learning by summarizing why these dialogues are so important. He explained, "Truth is not born nor is it to be found inside the head of an individual person, it is born between people collectively searching for truth, in the process of their dialogic interaction" (p. 110). Reading and meaning-making take place as co-constructions with others and invite students to explore additional perspectives and their evolving interpretations of texts and ideas.

A dialogical classroom is built on the interplay of multiple perspectives that engage students in this wrestle as they explore a range of opinions and ideas around an inquiry. These perspectives are valued not just in the reading of texts that reflect multiple cultures, but also in inviting students to consider the perspectives of others. As students learn to see conflicts and issues from multiple perspectives, they can develop more holistic views of situations and be better equipped to identify solutions.

Fishbowls, Socratic seminars, and classroom debates exemplify the type of strategies that create a space for students to share and listen to multiple perspectives on issues. These strategies encourage students to understand and explore a diversity of positions, thereby increasing students' ability to think critically. As students summarize, analyze, and evaluate arguments from different points of view, they broaden their perspectives and understanding of issues. Cultivating this ability proves key to not only to mastering the skills in the standards, but also to navigating the complex choices and situations they face in the world.

In addition, content-rich inquiries supplemented by intertextual experiences invite students to temporarily assume new roles, perspectives, and behaviors in sometimes imagined environments that support academic rigor, explore a diversity of perspectives, and harness the power of positive emotions crucial to learning (Immordino-Yang & Faeth, 2010). Earlier I cited neuroscience research explaining how engaged reading simulates what it's like to be another person (Wolf, 2018). For students who don't have feelings for books and cannot connect with texts in ways that engage them, dialogical strategies offer opportunities to help readers "try on" situations, feelings, and responses of the characters in the text through reading, re-reading, and re-creating the concepts and experiences. This helps them not only connect to the text, but also see other perspectives.

Crafting Dialogical Strategies

Taking a dialogical approach to reading comprehension allows students to integrate their experiences and understandings with texts, participate in real-world interactions related to the concepts they are studying, and bring their own lives into dialogue with the conflicts, characters, and themes in the literature. For students who find themselves disconnected from traditional approaches, dialogical strategies invigorate the content with alterity and variety. As I worked with the teachers featured in this book, we used these principles to create dialogical strategies to support the study of reading and literature in their classrooms. Correspondingly, we developed the following questions to guide us:

- ♦ Which themes, conflicts, questions, and challenges exist at the heart of the text and how do they show up in the lives of today's adolescents?
- ♦ What kinds of stimulating tasks might engage students in dialogue with the themes, conflicts, questions, and challenges in the text and anchor the reading experience?
- ♦ Where can formal and informal discussion provide opportunities for students to question, share understandings, and create connections to the content-rich material and their lives?
- ♦ How does the reading experience lend itself to exploring a diversity of perspectives, interpretations, and understandings?

Attending to these questions helped us create dialogical reading experiences that fostered situational interest among secondary students and motivated them to engage with the reading and literature. As a result, students engaged with one another, with texts, and with the world to explore a diversity of perspectives and to understand the content they studied.

The five chapters that comprise the rest of this book share examples from secondary ELA and reading teachers across the United States who used these dialogical principles to craft reading experiences to support students from a diversity of backgrounds and contexts. Each chapter includes succinct, accessible, and research-based explanations to illustrate specific stimulating tasks that helped students connect content to their lives and explore a diversity of perspectives.

Chapter 2 begins with an exploration of content-rich instruction crafted around artifactual inquiries, or opportunities for students to observe, interact with, and manipulate artifacts to build real-world connections to texts that engage students in the reading experience and help anchor their understandings. Next, Chapter 3 describes how simulations and shared experiences bring conflicts and themes to life while also building empathy and fostering diverse perspectives. Chapter 4 explores how dramatic and enactment strategies help students revisit texts to identify details that help them visualize, enact, and experience texts. Then Chapter 5 describes how integrating multiple dialogic strategies throughout a unit harnesses the social nature of learning and offers readers autonomy, relevance, and sociality—three components central to motivation. Finally, Chapter 6 offers a discussion of considerations and recommendations for teachers and instructional leaders seeking to implement these strategies.

Through a description of the whats, hows, and whys of each approach, supplemented by illustrations of practical applications of the approaches in secondary ELA classrooms, each chapter sketches out possibilities, considerations, and recommendations for teachers, instructional coaches, and school leaders. Where educational psychology research on reading motivation, neuroscience research on the reading brain, or research on reading comprehension supports these practices, it's included throughout the discussion. These examples are also supported by a discussion of variations of the strategies, as well as recommendations of both canonical texts and young adult titles that enrich the content focus of these inquiries.

Why This Matters

At the beginning of this chapter, I described the classical mythology application project Lieutenant Colonel Hupfer assigned to his students as an example of dialogic teaching and reading. But what I also appreciate is Colonel Hupfer's explanation of his motivation for giving the assignment. He emphatically (but perhaps unempathetically) states his rationale for requiring his students to read and study these myths and make connections to their own experiences. He explains:

> You're not kids anymore…The world around you is vast and complicated and it sure isn't going to wait for you to grow up. It's time to think seriously about your place in it.

His rationale struck me for a few reasons. First, because the last time I read through the standards—specifically those aimed at reading literary and informational texts—they covered skills such as identifying textual evidence, summarizing plots, and analyzing themes, characters, conflicts, and language. They ask students to determine central ideas, explain the relationship between claims, evidence, and reason, and to describe the influence of point of view. But they don't say anything about navigating the complexities of the world, let alone finding meaning or purpose in anything besides a text. And, at least as described by this ex-Marine-turned-English teacher, this purpose seems a little intense for 7th graders.

And yet, as adults and teachers we recognize that the world we inhabit—and that our students are inheriting—is one fraught with complications and complexities. Amidst the beautiful and the good are equal amounts of inequity and peril. There are different answers as to how one might deal with these uncertainties and, although we might not like Lieutenant Colonel Hupfer's tone, we realize that literature possesses the power to help students arrive at the very understandings the Lieutenant described. Our job as teachers involves not only teaching students how to read and engage with literature, but also facilitating meaningful opportunities to transact with texts that help them consider their own lives and experiences. For the teachers featured in the book, crafting dialogical strategies to help students transact with texts lies at the heart of teaching literature and reading. This is because participating in dialogical reading experiences engages students in both comprehending and connecting to texts, which is the kind of reading essential to their academic success and to their ability to think critically.

Whether in my former classroom, Lieutenant Colonel Hupfer's fictional classroom, or your future classroom, these approaches to learning typically demand more of students than they might be accustomed to when reading and recall questions are the norm. But they also raise the level of investment in the study of texts because they generate interest and help students discover the relevance of the themes, plots, conflicts, and characters in their own lives. Students identify connections to their own cultures and interests. Students liken moments in the text to their own challenges and experiences. They develop empathy for characters facing situations and conflicts unlike their own. Students cultivate a heightened attunement to the sensory imagery and connections to their current knowledge base and experience. At the heart of it, these strategies also get students engaged in meaningful dialogue—in dialogue with each other, in dialogue with the text, and in dialogue with the world around them.

References

Appleman, D. (2023). *Critical encounters in secondary English* (4th ed.). Teachers College Press.

Antonio, D. & Guthrie, J. (2008). Reading is social: Brining peer interaction to the text. In J. Guthrie (Ed.) *Engaging adolescents in reading* (pp. 49–63). Corwin.

Arnold, D., Lonigan, C., Whitehurst, G., & Epstein, J. (1994). Accelerating language development through picture book reading: Replication and extension to a videotape training format. *Journal of Educational Psychology*, 86(2), 235–243.

Aronson, B. & Laughter, J. (2016). The theory and practice of culturally relevant education: A synthesis of research across content areas. *Review of Educational Research*, 86(1), 163–206.

Aronson, E. (2002). Building empathy, compassion, and achievement in the jigsaw classroom. In J. Aronson (Ed.) *Improving academic achievement: Impact of psychological factors on education* (pp. 209–225). Academic Press.

Bakhtin, M. (1984). *Problems of Dostoevsky's poetics*. (C. Emerson, Trans). University of Michigan Press.

Baloche, L., Mauger, M, Willis, T., Filinuk, J. & Michalsky, B. (1993). "Fishbowls, creative controversy, Talking chips: Exploring literature cooperatively." *The English Journal*, 82(6), 43–48.

Beck, I. & McKeown, M. (2006). *Improving comprehension with questioning the author: A fresh and expanded view of a powerful approach*. Scholastic.

Berns, G. (2002). *The self-delusion: The new neuroscience of how we invent—and reinvent—our identities*. Basic Books.

Camp, D. (2000). It takes two: Teaching with twin texts of fact and fiction. *Reading Teacher*, 53(5), 400–408.

Clark, A., Anderson, R., Kuo, L., Kim, I., Archodidou, A., & Nguyen-Jahiel, K. (2003). Collaborative reasoning: Expanding ways for children to talk and think in school. *Educational Psychology Review*, 15(2), 181–198.

Dalton, B., Morocco, C., Tivnan, T. & Mead, P. (1997). Supported inquiry science: Teaching for conceptual change in urban and suburban science classrooms. *Journal of Learning Disabilities*, 30(6), 670–684.

Daniels, H. (2004). *Mini-lessons for literature circles*. Heinemann.

Douglass J. & Guthrie, J. (2008). Meaning is motivating: Classroom goal structures. In J. Guthrie (Ed.) *Engaging adolescents in reading* (pp. 17–32). Corwin.

Duke, N. & Pearson, P. (2002). Effective practices for developing reading comprehension. In Farstrup, A. & Samuels, S. (Eds.), *What research has to say about reading instruction* (3rd ed., pp. 205–242). International Reading Association.

Elfie, I. (2002). Examining multiple perspectives in literature. In Holden, J. & Schmit, J. (Eds.), *Inquiry and the literary text: Constructing discussions in the English classroom* (pp. 89–103). NCTE.

Fecho, B. (2011). *Writing in the dialogical classroom: Students and teachers responding to the texts of their lives.* NCTE.

Fink, R. (1995). Successful dyslexics: A constructivist study of passionate interest reading. *Journal of Adolescent & Adult Literacy, 39*(4), 268–280.

Fisher, D., Flood, J., Lapp, D. & Frey, N. (2011). Interactive read-alouds: Is there a common set of implementation practices? *The Reading Teacher, 58*(1), 8–17.

Fordham, N. (2006). Crafting questions that address comprehension strategies in content reading. *Journal of Adolescent and Adult Literacy, 49*(5), 390–396.

Freire, P. (1983). The importance of the act of reading. *The Journal of Education, 165*(1), 5–11.

Gay, G. (2010). *Culturally responsive teaching: Theory, research, and practice* (2nd ed.). Teachers College Press.

Gibb, R. & Guthrie, J. (2008). Interest in reading: Potency of relevance. In J. Guthrie (Ed.) *Engaging adolescents in reading* (pp. 83–98). Corwin.

Guthrie, J., Wigfield, A., & Perencevich, K. (Eds.) (2004). *Motivating reading comprehension: Concept-oriented reading instruction.* Lawrence Erlbaum.

Guthrie, J., Wigfield, A., Humenick, N., Perencevich, K., Taboada, A., & Barbosa, P. (2006). Influence of stimulating tasks on reading motivation and comprehension. *The Journal of Educational Research, 99*(4), 232–245.

Hagay, G., Peleg, R., Laslo, E., & Baram-Tsabari, A. (2012). Nature or nurture? A lesson incorporating students' interests in a high-school biology class. *Journal of Biological Education, 47*(2), 117–122.

Hidi, S., & Harackiewicz, J. M. (2000). Motivating the academically unmotivated: A critical issue for the 21st century. *Review of Educational Research, 70*(2), 151–179.

Immordino-Yang, H. & Faeth, M. (2010). The role of emotion and skilled intuition in learning. Mind, brain, & education. In D. Sousa (Ed.) *Neuroscience implications for the classroom* (pp. 69–83). Solution Tree Press.

Ivey, G. & Johnston, P. (2023). *Teens choosing to read: Fostering social, emotional and intellectual growth through books*. Teachers College Press.

Krapp, A., Hidi, S., & Renninger, K. (1992). Interest, learning, and development. In A. Krapp, S. Hidi & K. Renninger (Eds.). *The role of interest in learning and development*. (pp. 3–25). Lawrence Erlbaum.

Ladson-Billings, G. (1995). Toward a theory of culturally relevant pedagogy. *American Educational Research Journal, 32*(3), 465–491.

Mastropieri, M., Scruggs, T. & Magnusen, M. (1999). Activity-oriented science instruction for students with disabilities. *Learning Disability Quarterly, 22*(4), 240–249.

McRae, A. & Guthrie, J. (2009). Promoting reasons for reading: Teacher practices that impact motivation. In E. Hiebert (Ed.), *Reading more, reading better* (pp. 55–76). Guilford.

Nolen, S. B., & Nichols, J. G. (1994). A place to begin (again) in research on student motivation: Teachers' beliefs. *Teaching and Teacher Education, 10*(1), 57–69.

Palincsar, A. S., & Brown, A. L. (1984). Reciprocal teaching of comprehension fostering and monitoring activities. *Cognition and Instruction, 1*(2), 117–175.

Raphael, T. & McMahon, S. (1994). Book club: An alternative framework for reading instruction. *The Reading Teacher, 48*(2), 102–116.

Rosenblatt, L. M. (2005). *Making meaning with texts*. Heinemann.

Rodesiler, L., Lewis, M., & Brown, A. (2024). *Reading the world through sports and young adult literature: Resources for the English classroom*. NCTE.

Ross, J. A. (1988). Controlling variables: A meta-analysis of training studies. *Review of Educational Research, 58*(4), 405–437.

Schiefele, U. (2009). Situational and individual interest. In K. R. Wenzel & A. Wigfield (Eds.), *Handbook of motivation at school* (pp. 197–222). Routledge/Taylor & Francis Group.

Schmidt, G. (2023). *The labors of Hercules Beal*. Harper Collins.

Schoenbach, R., Braunger, J., Greenleaf, C., & Litman, C. (2003). Apprenticing adolescents to reading in subject-area classrooms. *Phi Delta Kappan, 85*(2), 133–138.

Taboada, A. Guthrie, J., & McRae, A. (2008). Building engaging classrooms: Motivating students daily. In R. Fink & S. J. Samuels (Eds.). *Inspiring reading success: Interest and motivation in an age of high-stakes testing* (pp. 141–166). International Reading Association.

Troyer, M. (2017). A mixed-methods study of adolescents' motivation to read. *Teachers College Record*, *119*(5), 1–48.

Wilkinson, I., & Son, E. (2011). A dialogical turn in research on learning and teaching to comprehend. In M. L. Kamil, P. D. Pearson, E. B. Moje, & P. P. Afflerbach (Eds.), *Handbook of reading research* (Vol. 4, pp. 359–387). Routledge.

Wolf, M. (2016). *Tales of literacy for the 21st century*. Oxford.

Wolf, M. (2018). *Reader, come home: The reading brain in a digital world*. Harper.

Zahorik, J. (1996). Elementary and secondary teachers' reports of how they make learning interesting. *Elementary School Journal*, *96*(5), 551–564.

Zhang, J., & Stahl, K. (2011). "Collaborative reasoning: Language-rich discussions for English learners." *The Reading Teacher*, *65*(4), 257–260.

2

Artifactual Inquiries

In San Antonio, Texas, as the thirty-one 9th graders from Abby Marchant's 5th period class made their way through the classroom door, only a few curiously eyed the black box. Those who did glanced at it warily, but amid the chatter and commotion most hardly noticed the latest classroom addition until after the bell rang, when Abby drew their attention to the front of the room. Once the class quieted down, Abby drew a large circle in the middle of the board with six smaller circles outside it, instructing the students to create a mind map by replicating the figure on their own papers. When she wrote "Romeo and Juliet" in the middle of the largest circle, they did too. Only then did most of them start to wonder: what about the box?

She then explained that the large black box in front of them contained items that represented key moments, themes, and symbols from the play. Then she invited students up to the front of the room to remove the items one by one. As each emerged Abby paused and explained, "Let's talk through words that come to mind when we think of this object" and the group brainstormed connections, predictions, and associations for each prop.

The first student pulled out a plastic toy sword. Before he could shout "En garde!," Abby wrote "sword" in the first of the six bubbles and asked, "What about the sword?" Students immediately made associations with death and duels and enemies, but Abby probed deeper. "But what drives someone to kill their enemies?" "Betrayal!," one student shouted. "War!," another yelled. With each additional word students shared, Abby added new bubbles extending from the original six on the whiteboard.

Then came a masquerade mask, what looked like strands of fake fire, and a corked bottle labeled "poison." Roberto quizzically asked "Poison? Isn't that a song? Like 'that girl is poison'?" To which Abby questioned back, "Yes! And what is that song trying to say?" Roberto lit up as he explained, "That the girl is toxic! And toxic people ain't worth your time!"

Someone removed a single red rose and the final student pulled out a string of star lights. Another student, Alonzo, pointed at them and asked, "Wait, isn't that like how Romeo and Juliet's love was written in the stars? And so, was theirs doomed?" Students tossed ideas back and forth across the classroom as Abby captured their ideas on the whiteboard. As the class reviewed the board, copied the notes, and reflected on their brainstorming, Mekela observed: "Miss, all of these objects have to do with death." But before Abby could respond, Jawan exclaimed, "Of course, they do—the play is a TRAGEDY. It's going to end tragically!"

The class laughed and together they read the prologue, with the students stopping to circle any words in the lines that made them think of the props and the terms they recorded on their mind maps (see Figure 2.1.).

As their exit ticket for the day the students drew pictures of the words they circled and described the connections and predictions they made between the prologue and the ideas recorded on their mind maps. This snapshot from Abby's classroom shows the power artifacts possess to motivate and engage readers from the very first day of the unit. Artifacts provide hands-on ways for students to build and access background knowledge, to make abstract concepts like symbol and theme concrete, and to integrate out-of-school identities into their learning. In each of these instances, objects ignite connection, interest, and relevance in ways that support comprehension and learning from texts.

This chapter explores how this dialogical learning approach provides one type of stimulating task that can trigger situational

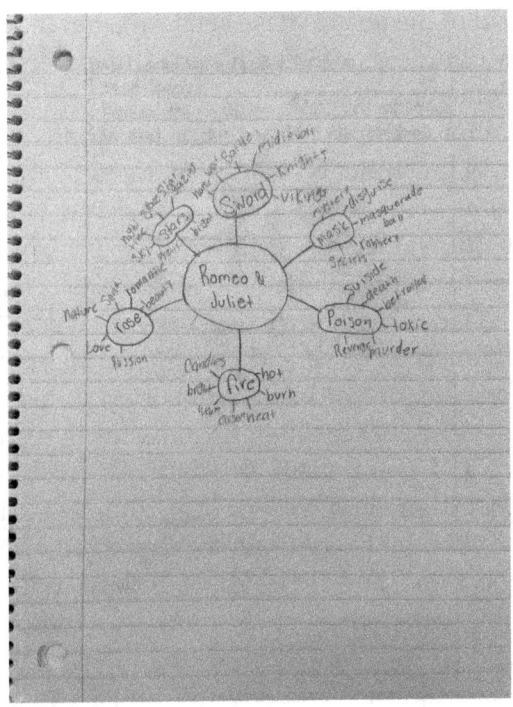

FIGURE 2.1 A mind map created by a student in Abby's class

interest and support comprehension, vocabulary growth, and the development of students' reader identities. These approaches engage students of all backgrounds and ability levels throughout the reading process by drawing connections between their lives and the characters, conflicts, and themes within the text that maximize comprehension and provide touchpoints for students to draw on in assessments of their learning.

What Makes Artifacts Dialogic?

Whether exploring props that represent symbols in a novel, examining objects to make inferences about characters in a play, or sharing trinkets representative of stories from their own lives, artifacts provide students with tangible touchstones for learning. Artifactual inquiries also facilitate lived experiences where objects from students' lives enter into dialogue with artifacts from the world of the text to make sense of what they read. These dialogical encounters are formative to students' understanding of and engagement with texts.

Artifacts offer multiple entry points into content-rich instruction that draws on students' lives, experiences, and interests to initiate dialogue with texts. When introduced before reading, artifacts help students access or build their background knowledge related to concepts, events, and ideas in texts (Guthrie et al., 2006; Swan, 2003). This knowledge proves central to situating students in relation to ideas and concepts at the beginning of a reading experience, but artifactual experiences also help establish touchpoints for students to return to during reading. As students observe and manipulate artifacts, real-world connections are formed between their experiences and texts (Douglass & Guthrie, 2008). Students continue to monitor their predictions, look for connections, and revise their understandings throughout the reading experience, anchoring their comprehension in these connections.

Artifactual inquiries embody the intertextual, hands-on learning approaches that trigger situational interest as readers interact with, interrogate, and manipulate concrete objects (Ekwueme et al., 2015; Renninger et al., 2019; Rutherford, 1993; Zahorik, 1996). The curiosity and excitement generated by artifacts help students deeply process information they encounter in texts and increase comprehension (Schiefele, 1999). Relatedly, artifacts also help make abstract ideas concrete by giving form and shape to concepts in the text, such as symbolism and vocabulary. These physical references prove particularly helpful for multilingual students working on associating concepts with the new vocabulary they are learning.

The artifacts themselves play a central, sensory role in learning because their smells, shapes, textures, appearances, and sounds evoke sensory experiences that support learning and engagement (Pahl & Roswell, 2010). As students take in information through multiple senses, the brain releases neurotransmitters that form new connections (or synapses) between neurons. These connections provide the building blocks for learning (Hannaford, 2007). Artifacts increase the number of senses engaged and the more senses activated in learning, the more synapses. And reading experiences that incorporate multi-sensory experiences support students with special needs (Kucirkova, 2024).

Artifactual inquiries also help teachers facilitate discussions where students and teachers co-construct understandings about texts and engage in questioning. Interacting with artifacts through hands-on experiences often leads to spontaneous questioning that motivates students to engage in genuine inquiry (Ross, 1988). As students work together to make inferences and connections about objects and their connections to plots, themes, and ideas in the text, they work with their teachers and with one another. As Pahl and Roswell (2010) explained,

> Artifactual literacy…widens what we understand to be the life-world experience of students and allows for a much more collaborative and participatory mode of teaching and learning to come into literacy education. Artifactual literacy is about exchange; it is participatory and collaborative, visual and sensory. It is a radical understanding of meaning making in a human and embodied way.
>
> (p. 134)

In these ways, artifacts provide the dialogical catalyst for creating opportunities for students to question, to learn from each other, and to work together to construct meaning.

On a personal level, artifacts also embody stories, experiences, and memories from students' daily lives. Objects from everyday experience serve a symbolic function, representing significant stories and experiences from students' cultures. Making space for artifacts from students' lives in the classroom "lets in the everyday" by acknowledging and validating "the material culture students inhabit out of school" making space for students' cultures, values, and identities in school (Pahl & Roswell, 2010, p. 11). Incorporating artifacts into classroom inquiries helps students share their stories about their identities, the identities of the characters they encounter, as well as meanings significant to other time periods, people, and cultures.

Applications and Examples of Artifactual Inquiry Strategies

The example from Abby's classroom that introduced this chapter illustrates the power of artifacts to facilitate dialogic reading experiences that generate situational interest in reading, support comprehension, and foster long-term individual interest. Gibb and Guthrie (2008) aptly summarized the power of hands-on, intertextual approaches highlighted in this chapter when they explained, "We want to involve students in seeing, hearing, touching, feeling, manipulating, and interacting concretely. These experiences create interest that can be linked to books" (p. 86). In addition to prop boxes, Jackdaws, time capsules, paper bag collages, shoebox autobiographies, and museum exhibits all use artifacts to ignite student interest and to prepare students to transact with the readings (see Table 2.1).

TABLE 2.1 Artifactual inquiries

Artifactual approach	*Before, during & after reading applications*
Prop box A compilation of artifacts that represent important plot points, themes, symbols, or elements of a text	**Before:** Students make predictions about relationships between the artifacts and possible symbols, events, characters, conflicts, and plot points in the text, then map these possibilities and/or write a scene using the props that can be acted out for the class. **During:** Throughout the study of the text both teacher and students return to the items as touchpoints to discuss evolving understandings of the significance of each item, checking and revising initial predictions and making new ones. **After:** Use as a tool to review the plot, development of symbols, and development of themes by returning to the artifacts at the conclusion of the text. Students may also select a single artifact and use it to guide a focused analysis of a theme, symbol, or character.

(Continued)

TABLE 2.1 (Continued)

Artifactual approach	Before, during & after reading applications
Jackdaws A collection of objects that represent important ideas, themes, concepts, vocabulary, or characters within a text or inquiry	**Before**: Activate students' background knowledge through exploration of objects related to the themes, concepts, vocabulary, and ideas essential to the inquiry. For students unfamiliar with concepts, vocabulary, and topics of the inquiry, these objects build background knowledge and helps make abstract ideas concrete. **During**: Throughout the unit the teacher references and encourages the students to reference the artifacts within the Jackdaws, linking them to conceptual knowledge, characters, vocabulary, and other elements of focus as they engage in the reading and study of the inquiry. **After**: Ask students to use the artifacts to help them create summaries of the text or answer the inquiry question. Students can also create their own Jackdaws that reflects their understandings of the setting or time period, scenes, or characters. Add an analysis component by asking them to include textual evidence and explanations for each item or trading with another student and using textual evidence to explain or support their explanation for each item.
Time capsule Artifacts that represent a time, place, person, or significant experience	**Before**: Help students access their background knowledge by brainstorming connections or answers to the inquiry question through listing or gathering artifacts they would include in a time capsule for the unit and explaining the rationale for their choices. **After**: Use as a summarizing strategy to represent significant people, events, symbols, experiences, words, or elements in the reading. It may also be used to represent development of characters, plots, or themes.

(Continued)

TABLE 2.1 (Continued)

Artifactual approach	Before, during & after reading applications
Shoebox autobiography Objects that represent facets of students' reader identities, as well as other important aspects of their identities	**Before**: At the beginning of the year students compile artifacts representative of their reader or learner identities, including objects that represent how they feel about reading, their biggest reading accomplishment, or their reading goals. They can also include items that symbolize other important aspects of their identities, challenges, and goals. **After**: At the conclusion of the semester or year, invite students to revisit their collections and add items that represent their biggest reading accomplishment that year, challenges they overcame, new interests or skills they developed, or their reading goals going forward.
Paper bag collage Images and artifacts assembled on the outside of a paper bag that represent a character's visible or outside characteristics and others inside the bag for inner or hidden qualities	**Before**: Make personal connections between the theme of appearance versus reality or character analysis by inviting students to think about their own identities—particularly in terms of those that are public and visible to others and those that are personal and not easy to see from outside. **During**: Throughout the reading of the text, keep track of how the characters present themselves to others—attributes others assume or infer from the character's physical characteristics, and observable talents, traits, and behaviors. Also note those things about the characters that others do not see—their inner qualities, values, challenges, and often surprise others or go unnoticed. **After**: Toward the end or after the reading, students share their paper bag collages and character or thematic analysis to support the images and items they chose for their paper bags.

(Continued)

TABLE 2.1 (Continued)

Artifactual approach	Before, during & after reading applications
Museum exhibit After students conduct research about details of the setting, topic, or other important background information, they exhibit and share their findings with one another	**Before**: Create a museum exhibit of artifacts that represent key concepts, ideas, background knowledge, and themes students will encounter in the text. As an introduction to the unit early on, invite students to browse the gallery and summarize their findings about each idea or concept. Or, ask students to make predictions based on the artifacts displayed that they can check and revise as they read. **After**: Begin the inquiry with one of the other artifactual strategies to orient students to the use of artifacts in the study of texts. As an after-reading strategy, students create an exhibit representing a theme, concept, vocabulary word within an inquiry unit or an answer to the essential question. They draw on textual evidence and their own analysis to craft an artist's statement explaining their exhibit. Their object and explanation become a part of a whole-class exhibit centered on the inquiry. This pairs nicely with the Jackdaws or prop box strategies to reflect student understanding of the reading and literature or with the shoebox autobiography to give students an opportunity to show their progress as readers or shifts in their reader identities.

But in each of these dialogical approaches, artifactual inquiry involves more than just bringing objects to class. Teachers can craft thoughtful and engaging inquiry experiences as they consider the role artifacts might play in the lives of students and in the texts they study (see Text Box 2.1).

Artifactual strategies are crafted to generate affective and cognitive engagement around a conflict, topic, theme, or idea central to a text. But these aren't just any texts. These are complex fiction and nonfiction texts embedded in content-rich instruction.

> **TEXT BOX 2.1 Creating Conditions to Maximize the Impact of Artifactual Inquiries**
>
> When considering ways to alter or combine artifactual inquiry approaches or to innovate and craft your own artifactual strategies and assessments, consider how the following questions might guide your planning:
>
> - What do students need to understand about the symbols, themes, conflict, or events in the text before, during, or after the reading?
> - In what ways do these symbols, themes, conflicts, or events overlap with students' cultures, values, and interests? What opportunities can I provide for students to identify these similarities and connections?
> - Which objects play a literal or symbolic role in the text?
> - Which of the artifactual strategies will invite students to connect the objects to their own background knowledge, emotions, and questions that will support their reading and interpretation of the text before reading?
> - Where might discussions and activities throughout the reading process provide touchpoints for students to use the prereading activity to help make sense of ideas in the text?

These artifactual strategies activate students' background knowledge and lead students to ask questions they genuinely want to understand as they engage with the text. When used in conjunction with comprehension routines, students participate in dialogue with their peers, with texts, and with their own lives as an extension of these experiences. The descriptions in the sections that follow highlight this kind of scaffolding and provide recommendations for implementing these strategies as a part of the reading experience.

Prop Box

The string of star lights, strands of fire, sword, masquerade mask, corked bottle of poison, and single red rose Abby compiled represent one approach to a prop box used to introduce and engage students in the study of a play. Prop boxes are collections of props, items, and resources that "represent significant symbols, conflicts, and characters of a given text" (Dulaney, 2012, pp. 38–39). Although fun to play with, these artifacts are more than just toys. They also provide an intertextual experience that generates situational interest and engagement in the reading.

A prop box is also a fantastic strategy to launch an inquiry unit and to introduce the inquiry question. When used before reading, prop boxes generate interest and launch students into the text by activating students' prior knowledge of, emotions related to, and experiences with the items to support students' comprehension of plots, symbols, and themes. Then, like Abby and her students, as students read, view, and examine the text, they make explicit connections between the prop box activity and the reading.

As teachers return to the objects throughout the study of the text, the objects also become touchpoints to check for understanding during the reading. For example, after reading Acts I and II of *Romeo and Juliet*, Abby returned to the prop box activity to help students make concrete connections between the objects the class had looked at, touched, and thought about at the beginning of the inquiry and the events, characters, and themes they just read about. She offered prompts such as "Look at your maps and think, 'What were some of the ideas and predictions you generated when you explored the prop box?' Which of those came true and which need to be revised?" Then she invited students to return to their mind maps and to discover which of the words, predictions, and ideas they initially identified had come to pass. Students talked with their partners and revised their predictions based on evidence from the text. Then students wrote down a prediction about what would happen in the remainder of the play, using at least two words from their mind maps.

When they continued to work their way through the drama, characters also became an important part of these discussions as the class linked them to the items in the prop box. When the class wrote, talked about, or noticed themes or characters related to the items, Abby purposely pointed back to the objects to ground the students' thinking in the physical objects. Throughout the unit students revisited and reviewed the themes, piecing together the roles each character played in the unfolding events and the significance of each of the symbols. Periodically Abby invited students to turn and talk about which objects were not present and to make predictions about what might happen next based on the items that still hadn't shown up in the text.

At the conclusion of their reading, Abby wanted her students to share what they learned about the relationships between the characters and the events in the play. Because her school and district required the unit's final assessment to mirror the format of the state writing test, Abby crafted the following writing prompt for the final assessment of this unit:

> Select one character from *Romeo and Juliet* and his/her key moment in the play to discuss. Explain what the key moment in the play reveals about the character and his/her connection to a major theme of the play.

The prop box activity at the beginning of the unit primed students to attend to important happenings in the play, particularly those that involved the props. As they continued their reading, the objects became associated with events and the events with characters. As a result, many students wrote about the characters in the play in relation to the significant moments or themes the students had tracked on their own throughout their reading. In their essays students incorporated the evidence from the text, which they also drew from their reading notes and analyses.

Although Abby's students took a more traditional approach to assessment, prop boxes offer other assessment possibilities as well. For example, teachers could invite students to compile their own props and create a box containing items that represent plot points in the story, a character in the text, or evidence of a theme within the text. Then students could write paragraphs that explain why they included each item, supported by textual evidence. Or students could create prop boxes and then give them to another student who would then create an explanation for each item, complete with textual evidence to support their interpretation.

One of the most appealing features of a prop box is that it works with almost any text where a study of themes, symbols, motifs are central to the inquiry. Although the items included will vary from text to text, prop boxes can be used with literary works, such as novels, short stories, poems, graphic novels, plays, chapters from novels, and novels in verse. A cross, a baby bracelet, a notebook, a poem, and merengue music might be a part of a prop box for *The Poet X*. A basketball, a dictionary, a ring, and a family picture could be included in a prop box for *The Crossover*. But prop boxes also work with nonfiction texts, including literary nonfiction, creative nonfiction, essays, and even historic documents. A stone, the novel *To Kill a Mockingbird*, a piece of metal, a gavel, and a book of hymns might be just a few of the objects included in a prop box for the young reader's edition of *Just Mercy*. In each instance objects prompt students to question, make predictions, and read the text with a curiosity and a focus on major images, symbols, and ideas.

Variations on a Prop Box: Jackdaws

Like prop boxes, Jackdaws are collections of objects, music, articles, texts, recordings, and other artifacts found in or associated with a story. Popular in early elementary grades, these collections may be presented before reading a text to stimulate interest or build background knowledge, during a reading experience to support comprehension, or at the conclusion of a reading experience to reflect on connections and information learned (Strickland, 2005). Incorporating and referencing items from the Jackdaw collection throughout the study of a text provides students with opportunities to make tangible connections to concepts and increase student engagement with ideas and concepts in the text (Dowd, 1990). They also increase student interest and engagement in discussions about literature (Rasinski, 1983).

What differentiates Jackdaws from prop boxes is their less structured use as a tool to broadly introduce readers to unfamiliar elements in the reading, such as settings and vocabulary. For example, to help readers more specifically understand a historical period, a teacher might create a Jackdaw using artifacts of the period which includes maps, recipes, sheet music or songs, advertisements, magazines, letters, artwork, tools, documents from the time, labels, posters, tickets, playbills, and other items (Dowd, 1990). Students learn more about background information about the time period from examining these artifacts, but they don't necessarily use them to produce an analysis of the text.

But Jackdaws also initiate dialogue between secondary readers and the settings, background information, and contexts of fiction or nonfiction texts. They could also be created as collections of items that provide insights about a character or event. For example, a map of the city of Birmingham, a list of Alabama Jim Crow laws, images of the segregated city, a Bible, and a toy nightstick might prepare students to better understand the setting of *Letters to Birmingham Jail*. Or collections of items could be used to help students bridge vocabulary words with concepts before, during, or after an inquiry unit.

Time Capsules

The term "time capsule" was coined by a publicist from Westinghouse Electric and Manufacturing Company attempting to describe a tube 90 inches long and 9 inches in diameter that the company created for the 1939 New York World's Fair, designed to be buried 50 feet below the surface of Flushing Meadows-Corona Park, and not to be opened until the year 6939 (Sterbenz, 2014). But more interesting than the tube itself was its purpose: to preserve relics of life in the US from the time for future inhabitants of the planet. These items included a fountain pen, alphabet blocks, a toy truck and a toy doll, cigarettes, and seeds.

In addition to these items, the time capsule also contained a swath of literary artifacts, including a microfilm with ten million words and a thousand pictures, newsreels, a copy of the Bible, a Sears Roebuck catalog, a dictionary, an almanac, and a letter from Albert Einstein.

This famous example illustrates what a time capsule is—a collection of artifacts preserved in a contained space—as well as its purpose—to represent a time, place, group of people, or significant experience worth sharing with people in the future. Like prop boxes, time capsules offer students opportunities to use artifacts as a starting point for engaging in dialogue about people, places, events, and ideas together as they explore the significance of these items in relation to the texts and inquiry in question. And the wide variety of materials often included in time capsules expands the sensory experience to sounds, images, and textures of a time.

If asked to hypothesize about why people of the past would preserve these objects for people in the future, students could explore the symbolic nature of each object and connect it to what they know or uncover about the events, values, and people of the time. But the reverse is also true: students could create a time capsule that included symbolic artifacts to demonstrate their understanding of a time, place, person, or significant experience.

When Marion launched the inquiry "What Does It Mean to be an American?" with her 11th graders in Albuquerque, New Mexico, she asked her students to gather in small groups to create a time capsule to be opened 1 million years from now that would showcase Americans in 2023 and what defined American culture. They began by brainstorming possible objects and then, as a group, identified and illustrated the six artifacts that they felt epitomized what it meant to be an American in 2023. Next, they wrote a one-sentence explanation of the symbolism behind each object.

The groups busied themselves generating ideas as Marion walked around the classroom, eying their posters curiously. Some of the objects seemed to carry obvious significance or connections—for example, almost every poster included a cell phone or some type of social media icon. But what did Miley

Cyrus have to do with the US? Other items, such as MAGA hats, Pride flags, and images of guns, made Marion a bit uncertain as to where the discussions might lead.

But Marion also trusted her students and as each group presented, the rest of the class listened and took notes about what the artifacts suggested about modern-day Americans. One by one groups shared their posters. One included a gun, a Barbie, a medical mask, a cell phone, cash, and a world on fire. The phone represented the human obsession with screens, the essential nature of phone in communication, and the way it's difficult to participate in society without a phone.

More than one group also pointed out that the worldwide connections made possible by phones extended America's reach beyond our soil and made the world a global space that defied physical borders. The medical mask nodded to the impact of COVID on the world as well as the way the pandemic restrictions shaped the way people engaged with one another. Marion initially expected more superficial responses with celebrities, but students explained people like Miley Cyrus represented their generation's desire to rebel and push back against social norms, which was also characteristic of the nation at this time. As students discussed more politically charged items, they used them not to represent personal beliefs, but to reflect the polarization of a society filled with discord and disagreement around politics.

After the presentations, the whole class discussed the following questions:

- Which words or values repeatedly came up during the presentations?
- If you had to list the three most important values for Americans today, what would those be?
- Are these the best values for a country to put first? Why or why not?

As the class explored these questions, Marion listed their ideas on the whiteboard.

Next, the discussion segued to the values at the time of the drafting of the United States' foundational documents and the founding fathers. Marion asked the students to consider which of the words or values they originally listed would also represent what the founding fathers valued and students circled those. Then she asked them which represented words or values the founding fathers would have disagreed with and asked students to draw a line through those.

As the class shared their rationales for the words they kept or dismissed, their comments and questions pointed to differences in present and past US culture, beliefs, and practices. They also interrogated the values of the time period, the practices of people and groups, as well as the differences between ideals in the documents of this era and the realities of their practices. Armed with this foundation, students entered their discussions and explorations of the Declaration of Independence, the Preamble of the Constitution, and the Bill of Rights with background knowledge and critical questions to guide their reading.

Time capsules can also be used after reading to assess student mastery of setting, characters, themes, or ideas. In this example from Marion's classroom, she asked students to consider values from the modern era in relation to those from the time period and ideologies of foundational US documents. But time capsules can also be used to explore themes in canonical and contemporary texts that interrogate loss, triumph, relationships, and identity. Texts that work well with time capsules include those where characters explore issues of identity, such as *In the Wild Light, Me Moth, Starfish,* or *Piecing Me Together*. Others, such as *Breakout* feature students creating time capsules as a part of the narrative itself. Or consider a genre approach. Dystopian texts such as *The Giver, Unwind, Fahrenheit 451,* or a collection of short stories featuring pieces like "Harrison Bergeron," "The Lottery," and "All Summer in a Day," might inspire interesting time capsules that showcase students' understandings of the setting, conflicts, and characters in these works, as well as the unique restrictions or features of their worlds. Another approach might ask students to include current modern objects that would be considered irrelevant or might be extinct in the dystopian worlds of these texts. Consider the relevance of a bulletproof vest in the world of *Scythe*. Which items might be unnecessary in *The Hunger Games* or *The Giver*?

With these and countless other themes, students can compile time capsules that represent characters, conflicts, and pivotal events that shape the themes and ideas in a text. Students can also include captions or paragraphs explaining each of the items they chose to include (Knecht, 2021). Imagine a time capsule that represented the transition of characters in middle school to high school or from high school into the adult world—such as *Hearts Unbroken, The Serpent King*, or *The Outsiders*. As students consider the various items added to the time capsule, they can also be challenged to think about the type of container they would use and how that might also reflect the meaning and significance of the theme or topic.

Variations on Time Capsules: Video Time Capsules

One middle school teacher described creating a video time capsule by filming footage of his students throughout their 7th grade year together that he then compiled into a VHS and hid in the high school trophy case until their senior year, providing visual evidence of students' growth and advancement toward their goals (Lonberger & Lonberger, 1995). Although VHS may be a technology of the past, the concept of creating an artifact that documents growth over time is still very relevant. For teachers seeking to capture similar growth in their students' literacy skills, abilities, and goals, capturing footage at the beginning of the semester can help illustrate students' literacy identities that they can then view and reflect on at the end of the year. But students could also create their own video time capsules for characters in a play or novel or real people from nonfiction texts.

Variations on Time Capsules: Reverse Time Capsules

In 1995 *Wired* magazine featured an article describing a "reverse time capsule" that, instead of containing present-day artifacts of significance for the future, would include a collection of artifacts from the present day that might astound people from past generations. Already adapted to an essay assignment (Coulter, 2001), the reverse time capsule possesses possibilities for the study of literature as well. At the conclusion of a text, challenge students to consider which items, if placed in a reverse time capsule, might have changed the outcome of the story. Invite students to explain how each item would shift the narrative and alter the plot for good or for ill. For example, consider the items that might be literal game changers in novels like *Ethan Frome*, *The Book Thief*, or *Salt to the Sea*.

Variations on Time Capsules: Online Capsules

The Andy Warhol Museum in Pittsburgh, Pennsylvania features a few online time capsules that patrons can view from anywhere in the world on the museum's website. Gen Z is the focus of one exhibit that includes images of artifacts submitted by individuals, including the artwork, pets, social media, current events, fashion, music, technology, and sports that represent this generation. Another part of the website features community time capsules containing images of cultural representations of the German American, African American, Italian American, and Russian American immigrant groups who made the areas around Pittsburgh their home. Both these online time capsules exemplify the types of online time capsules a class or group of classes could create by assembling images of artifacts that represent various answers to an essential question like Marion's "What does it mean to be an American?"

Shoebox Autobiographies

Dialogic approaches to teaching reading and literature include not only content-rich discussions about texts and inquiry questions, but also the reader. Typically, this means bringing the reader's background, knowledge, interests, and experiences into dialogue with the text as well as with others. But these approaches also put readers in dialogue with their many identities and, when it comes to reading, one of the most important identities to consider is a student's reader identity.

Matti, a 7th grade reading teacher at a Title I junior high in Utah, wanted to help her students improve their abilities to fluently read and comprehend text as well as to wrestle with vocabulary as they studied engaging fiction and nonfiction texts. But she also wanted to help her students think critically about their reader identities—both how they saw themselves as readers now and who they wanted to be as readers when they left the class. For Matti, the artifacts compiled in shoebox autobiographies provided a meaningful tool to help students begin to reposition their reader identities (Pahl & Roswell, 2010) and build classroom community at the beginning of the semester as students shared their literacy practices and interests.

Matti introduced the assignment by defining a shoebox autobiography as a collection of items that represent who students are as readers and individuals (Moore & Onofrey, 2007). These collections of artifacts differ from the others previously described because they inspire dialogue among students about themselves and their identities as readers. They too can include sensory objects and experiences to share, and they make concrete some of the most important abstract concepts influencing students' learning and development: their reader and individual identities.

After introducing the concept of a shoebox autobiography, Matti then shared the three required items they needed to include an object that represented how the student felt about reading; an object that represented the student's biggest reading accomplishment; and an object that represented one thing the student wanted to improve as a reader (see Figure 2.2).

These typically included things traditionally associated with literacy, such as favorite or first books, pieces of their own writing, or writing that they admire by authors. But she also asked students to include three other objects that represented other important parts of their identities. These might reflect their family culture, challenges they've overcome, favorite hobbies, goals, or past achievements—objects such as photographs, images, music, lyrics, video games and other items representative of the identities important to them.

Matti then modeled the assignment by sharing her own shoebox with students. For example, she included Elizabeth Acevedo's novel *With the Fire on High* to represent her biggest

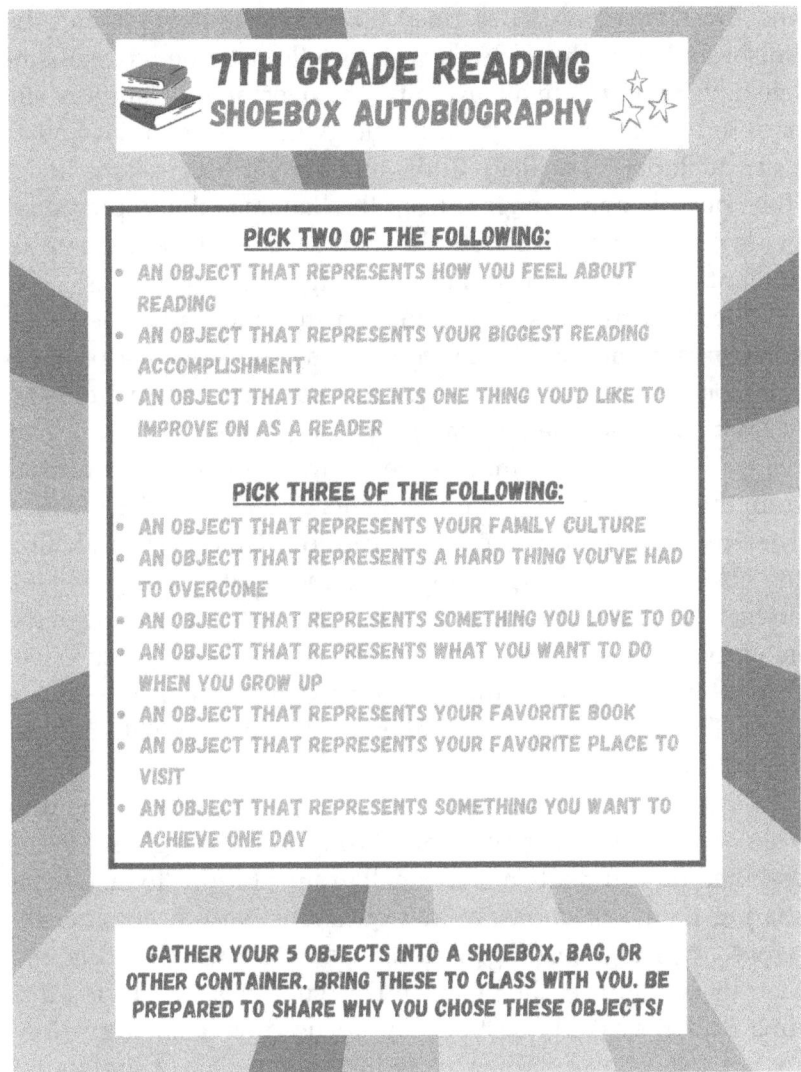

FIGURE 2.2 Assignment sheet for the 7th grade reading shoebox autobiography

reading accomplishment. Matti explained that she hadn't considered herself a reader for a long time, but when she took a young adult literature class she read *The Poet X* (another book by the same author), which made her fall in love with reading again and led her to read this book too. She also included her graduation cap to symbolize her biggest reading accomplishment. To her the graduation cap symbolized accomplishment and pride and those two words described how Matti felt every time she finishes a book. She added a water bottle from her college athlete days to represent a hard thing she overcame—a surgery she endured after she got hit in the face with a softball. Her other items included Hawaiian Tropic moisturizer because she loved to be outside and a magnet from the Bahamas that represented her favorite place to visit. As she shared each of these items with students, Matti explained their meanings and connections.

She then invited students to brainstorm ideas for their own shoebox autobiographies by considering the same list of questions on the assignment sheet. Students included five objects, at least two from the first category that directly related to their reader identity. Next, they chose no more than three prompts from the second that explore elements of their broader identity. They recorded their responses as captions for each item, listing the object and then explaining the reasons why they chose the object (see Figure 2.3). In the days leading up to the sharing of the autobiographies, Matti read the responses, asked questions to prompt further details, and invited students to revise their captions. This read-through also allowed her to vet what students would share.

Once students compiled their objects, they placed them in a shoebox or other container and brought them to class. On the assigned day students met in small groups of four to take turns sharing their collections, asking questions, and discussing different ways that reading, writing, and experiences influenced their lives. Matti set the timer for three minutes and during that time students asked questions and focused on a single speaker. Arturo's shoebox autobiography included a pair of glasses for his first item because he used glasses to read and to focus his eyes, but also because he set a goal for the class to better focus as a reader (see Figure 2.4).

Another student, Michael, included a spider for his first object because he disliked both spiders and reading. However, the second object he included was the first book in a five-book series that he enjoyed—or at least considered "bearable." The captions helped each speaker stay focused and the questions asked by other students helped the speaker elaborate.

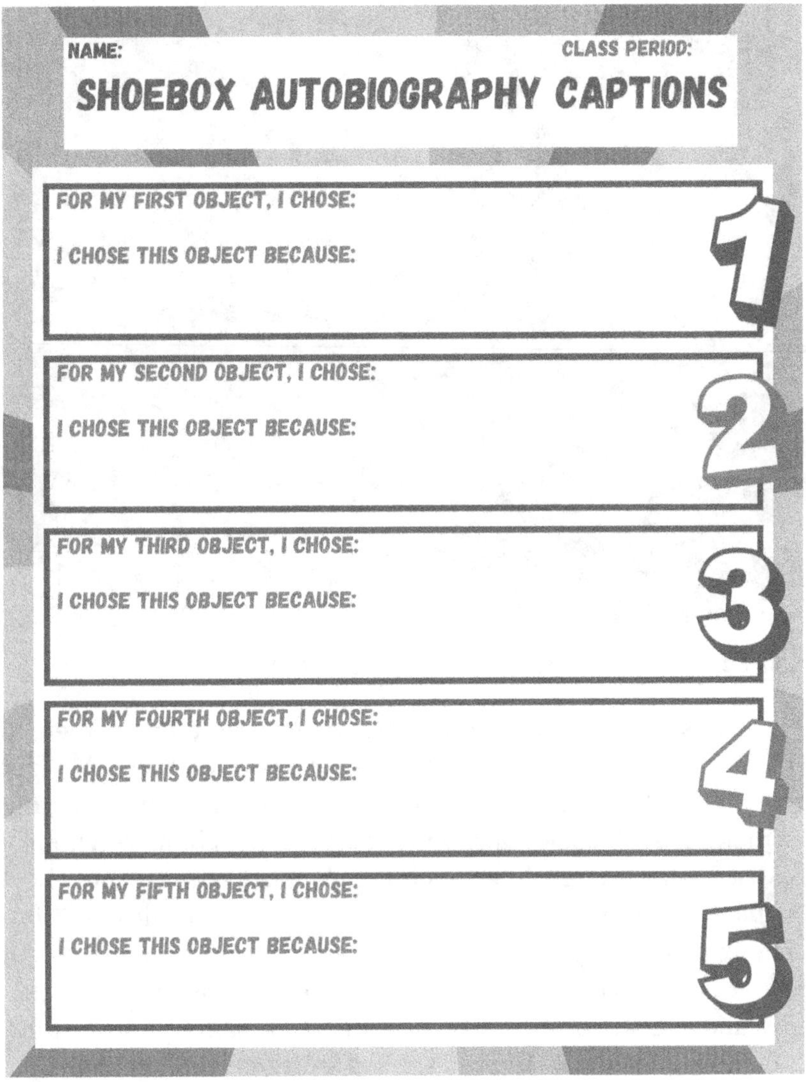

SHOEBOX AUTOBIOGRAPHY CAPTIONS

NAME: CLASS PERIOD:

1. FOR MY FIRST OBJECT, I CHOSE:
   I CHOSE THIS OBJECT BECAUSE:

2. FOR MY SECOND OBJECT, I CHOSE:
   I CHOSE THIS OBJECT BECAUSE:

3. FOR MY THIRD OBJECT, I CHOSE:
   I CHOSE THIS OBJECT BECAUSE:

4. FOR MY FOURTH OBJECT, I CHOSE:
   I CHOSE THIS OBJECT BECAUSE:

5. FOR MY FIFTH OBJECT, I CHOSE:
   I CHOSE THIS OBJECT BECAUSE:

FIGURE 2.3 Template for the shoebox autobiography captions

When the timer went off, the students rotated to the next speaker. At the conclusion of the activity Matti invited the whole class to debrief and talk about what they learned from the experience, both about themselves as readers as well as about their classmates. They also discussed the implications of these realizations for future work in their class.

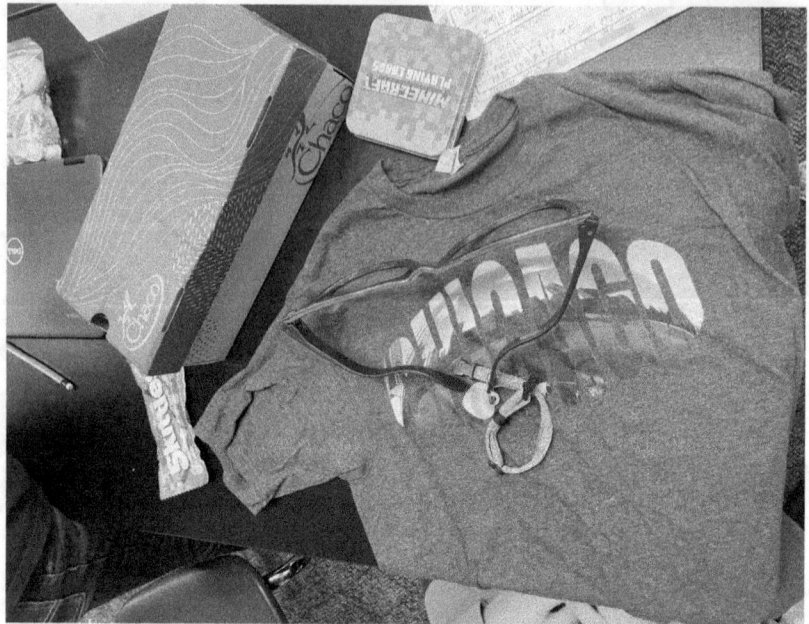

FIGURE 2.4 Photograph of a sample shoebox autobiography

Most students enjoyed the strategy because it allowed them to share about themselves at a time of the year when they felt eager or anxious about getting to know their classmates and wanting to make friends. They also enjoyed learning about previously undiscovered shared interests among their peers. Ultimately, it enabled Matti to introduce the idea of reader identities in a concrete way and helped students see the nuances of their different reader selves. This activity also provided a catalyst for discussion about goal setting—as it pertained to reading goals in fluency, vocabulary development, word study, and comprehension, and also to their reader identities.

Variations on a Shoebox Autobiography: The Paper Bag Collage

Like the shoebox autobiography, paper bag collages create a space for students to parts of themselves with their classmates. Paper bag collages about characters allow students to engage in analysis of character traits, motives, and values while exploring themes of appearance versus reality (Prince William Network, 1997).

To introduce the assignment, begin by instructing students to collect artifacts and images that represent themselves and their identities—both how they see themselves and how they think they are seen by others. Next, ask students to sort their collections into two categories: the images and items that represent the way others see them and more-commonly-known elements of their lives and those artifacts that represent less-known or more internal parts of themselves. Requiring four or five artifacts on the inside and the same number on the outside provides a nice balance without overwhelming the students or their groups. Additionally, requiring at least two of the items to relate to their reader identity will help students begin thinking about how their literacy habits intersect with these other elements of their lives.

Students should then secure or attach the first pile of artifacts to the outside of a paper bag, placing the images and objects that represent the less-known parts of themselves inside the bag. On the designated day, students bring their paper bag collages to class to share with small groups of their peers. After sharing, ask students to reflect in writing about what they learned by viewing their classmates' collages. This activity lends itself to examining differences between appearances and realities as well as the different ways reading plays a formative role in identity.

About halfway through the texts, students should select a character and create another paper bag collage—this time collecting images and items that represent the character. Once again, they will sort the items into two categories: the outside characteristics that other characters see and project on the character and then items that represent the inner complexities of the character that others don't recognize or readily acknowledge. Students then attach the objects on the corresponding parts of the bag, representative of the character's visible and unseen qualities. As they share the character paper bag collages with their peers, they should also consider what role these differences play in the character's development, their ability to wrestle with conflicts in the story, and their growth in relation to the themes. When integrated with a study of texts that examine themes of prejudice and judgment, this assignment invites students to question the assumptions they make about others as well as differences between appearances and realities.

One aspect that distinguishes this strategy from other artifactual approaches is its specific focus on characterization and theme. When teaching characterization, ask students to collect textual evidence of characters' external and internal qualities. Then, as they consider the evidence, brainstorm images and objects that illustrate these qualities. In small groups they can collectively assemble a paper bag collage for a character in the novel and then share their collections with the larger class.

Paper bag collages pair nicely with texts that consider appearance versus reality like *The Outsiders, The Great Gatsby, Macbeth*, or *The Hate U Give*. Imagine a paper bag collage for Ponyboy, Lady Macbeth, Daisy, or Maverik Carter that helps students discover the complexities between these characters' outward displays in society and their inner motivations or hidden desires. Paper bag collages can also be used to help students consider the challenge of truly knowing another person and the complications of making judgments about others based on external features, such as in texts like *To Kill a Mockingbird, The Merchant of Venice, Ghost, Speak*, or *Hamlet*. What might a paper bag collage representing Boo Radley, Portia, Castle "Ghost" Crenshaw, Melinda, or Ophelia include?

Museum Exhibit

At the Smithsonian National Museum of American History Miss Piggy and Kermit the Frog currently reside in an exhibit dedicated to "American Stories." Under the glow of lights and a giant quote attributed to Kermit himself that reads "If life were easy, it wouldn't be difficult," this famous couple sits, frozen in 1976. Their placement here represents both the debut of these iconic characters as well as what the plaque beside them describes as "fourth wall-breaking" performances aimed at promoting laughter as well as strength among differences.

Whether at a place as vast as the Smithsonian or within the walls of a middle school classroom, museum exhibits offer opportunities to dialogue with artifacts. In these spaces artifacts serve as symbols to represent significant ideas, themes, and motifs in the world, in texts, and in students' own lives. Here participants enter sensory experiences where the sights, sounds, images, and even smells of the artifacts facilitate dialogue with ideas that words alone do not. Although each of the artifactual inquiries described thus far ignite curiosity, access readers' background knowledge of topics to prepare them for the reading experience, and provide an anchor to this knowledge throughout the inquiry, artifacts can also play a role in summative representations of students' understandings of themselves and of literature. Museum exhibits are powerful tools to make this happen.

In the previous section I described the way Matti used shoebox autobiographies to help students explore their reader identities at the beginning of the semester. To provide them with a way to reflect on their growth at the end of the semester, Matti designed a museum exhibit that showcased their triumphs and successes as readers.

To begin, students participated in writing stations where they reflected on three separate questions: "What was your biggest challenge as a reader that you overcame this semester?," "How did you grow the most as a reader?," and "What was your biggest reading accomplishment?" After completing the stations, Matti taught a minilesson about representation and students answered two more questions: "Describe one item that represents who you are as a reader" and "How does this item relate to who you've become as a reader this semester?"

Like before, Matti reviewed students' responses and helped them expand on or refine their ideas. Some needed to clarify ties between the object and their captions; others needed more details. In class, students then revised final drafts of these responses into captions that would accompany their item on display and typed and printed them. As they left class, they committed to bringing in their artifacts on the second to last day.

On the appointed day Matti arranged the room so each student had space to display their object and captions. As students entered the room, they received comment cards that they could fill out in response to the displays and give feedback to their peers. The comment cards included three different prompts: "Something positive I liked about this display was…," "A book I would recommend for you is…," and "This exhibit inspired me to…" all designed to help students enter into dialogue about their reactions and understandings from one another's displays.

Once each student's display was ready, the class began walking around the room to view one another's exhibits. As students read the captions and looked at the artifacts selected, they noted the symbolism in one another's displays. For example, Ellie's display featured a speaker, and in her description she explained how the speaker represented how much her reading out loud improved. She shared, "I used to have a hard time with my grammar and pronouncing certain words or names out loud. It also describes how I am more willing to read out loud in front of people." In response to the question about her biggest reading accomplishment she wrote

> Reading out loud was my biggest reading accomplishment. Practicing more reading out loud helped me get more comfortable with it. Reading in groups helped me get better with my fluency and pronunciation. So I think that this year I improved a lot with reading out loud.

Ellie's improvement as a fluent reader also showed up in her test scores, but her description of her increased confidence provided insight for her peers. In their feedback one of her peers responded to the "This exhibit inspired me to…" comment card by remarking, "…read out loud more. I have a hard time reading out loud too. It's nice to see that someone else has that problem."

Katrina, another student in the class, brought in a rock as her object, explaining that just like rocks, reading is hard. She went on to describe the need to "read every day to build up your reading tolerance," and then detailed how she went from reading only 5 minutes a day to 40 minutes to an hour by the end of the class. In her caption describing her biggest reading accomplishment she stated:

> I think the biggest reading accomplishment is when you go to "i don't like books i have no goals and i get bored in 1 minute and [i] don't really care about books and reading" to "i love reading i read everyday for 20 minutes i have a goal to read for 50 minutes today." When I started this class I didn't care about reading but when I started reading the good books and understanding the books I started enjoying the class.

For Katrina, Ellie and so many other students in the class, the museum exhibit provided a space for them to reflect on and display their growth as readers in words as well as in tangible artifacts. Students wrote their feedback in response to the prompts on the comment cards, then left the card at the exhibit and made their way to the next display. As students in the class viewed and interacted with each exhibit they engaged in conversations with one another, but they also entered into dialogue with the exhibits and the exhibit creators with their comments and questions.

In more text-based summative assessments featuring museum exhibits, students use artifacts to represent answers to essential questions and to reflect their analysis of texts (Coombs & Freeze, 2018). Instead of selecting an object that represents students' own growth, museum exhibits can feature objects that represent the growth of characters throughout the text, symbols within the text, or the development of themes. For example, when Mercedes' 11th grade class read Gene Luen Yang's graphic novel *American Born Chinese*, they created a museum exhibit around the theme of culture and ancestors (see Figure 2.5). These exhibits helped students consider the connections and tensions they felt within their own cultures, which they then drew on and explored as they read the book and watched Danny navigate his own.

In these displays students also prepare a written component, but instead of crafting reflection questions about their own growth, they anchor the description and response in the text.

> **Culture Gallery**
>
> As we've been reading *American Born Chinese*, we have discussed and analyzed the objects and symbols used throughout the text that represent Jin Wang's culture and identity. Through symbols and objects in one's life, we can better understand who we, and others, are.
>
> Your Task: Using the questions you answered on the back side of the cultural Venn diagram, choose one question for your focus. Choose an object that represents your answer to that question and write a museum label (using the must have/could have list we made in class) describing the object, any cultural/identity significance it has to you, and why you chose it. Then, on the date of the gallery display, bring the object to display along with your label.
>
> Questions to consider:
> - What do you know about your ancestors?
> - What's something about your culture/who you are that you're proud of?
> - How does your family preserve traditions/culture?
> - Where do you feel like you most fit in?
>
> Objects can be an image, artwork, food, or anything that represents your answer to any of the questions above.
>
> Date of the gallery display: _____

FIGURE 2.5 Cultural gallery assignment sheet

For example, written responses might draw on textual evidence to explain how the object represents the answer to the guiding inquiry questions that frame the unit. Or they might include quotes from the text itself to support the description of how the object symbolizes the growth of characters or the development of a theme.

Like Matti's class, on the day of the exhibit students should display their objects and writeups as well as take time to view and respond to the displays of their classmates. Comment cards, whole-class discussions, or reflections offer opportunities for students to dialogue about what they learned from one another as well as what the displays mean for their own understandings.

Variations on Museum Exhibits: Examining Setting & Culture

If an understanding of the setting is important to comprehending the story, a museum exhibit could also be used as a before-reading strategy to help students research and teach one another about the historical background of a time or setting. Assign students a topic to research related to the setting, topic, or other important information in the text and ask them to create an exhibit with an artifact and a brief description explaining the significance of that element to help build their background knowledge (Yedinak, n.d.).

This type of exhibit might feature day-to-day objects that give clues about the era, such as advertisements, popular magazines, clothing, foods, catalogs, sports, and other entertainment or features of the location, similar to those features in *The Smithsonian Museum Magazine* "101 Objects that Made America" (Kurin, 2013). Then invite students to participate in a gallery walk to examine the artifacts and learn about the context of the time period from one another's displays. This approach can be particularly helpful when preparing students to read historical fiction or nonfiction texts when a strong grasp of the setting is important to the conflict, themes, and development of the novel.

Considerations

The artifactual approaches described in this chapter offer a handful of ways teachers engage students with abstract ideas by grounding them in tangible artifacts throughout a unit of study.

As teachers consider the themes, conflicts, and motifs in specific texts, these strategies might be adapted and tailored to the unique contexts of the texts they teach. For example, students who read *March* by John Lewis and Andrew Aydin might assemble a collection of scrapbook items that John would find essential in telling his story. Students reading *To Kill a Mockingbird* might consider which artifacts Boo could hide in the hollowed-out tree to represent the transition from innocence the children experience in the book. Readers of Jacqueline Woodson's verse novel *Brown Girl Dreaming* could assemble a suitcase of items Woodson would have kept from her childhood to represent significant moments in the narration. Or, after reading *The Giver* students could assemble memory boxes with artifacts that represent essential memories in the characters' development throughout the novel.

Whether creating your own or tailoring one of the examples in this chapter to the context of your classroom, the strongest artifactual inquiries share a few characteristics in common. First, they typically involve a stimulating hands-on experience that generates situational interest in the context of the content and expands students' background knowledge. As a part of the experiences, students individually and collectively generate questions that drive the inquiry. But just as central to the engagement is a high-quality text. During their reading—both on their own and with their peers—dialoguing with high-quality texts invites students to make explicit connections between the artifacts and the themes, topics, conflicts, and characters. In these readings students use textual evidence to make explicit connections between the artifacts and the text to support and expand students' comprehension.

Steven Lubar and Kathleen Kendrick (n.d.), affiliated curators with the Smithsonian, challenge students and educators to think about artifacts as objects that tell stories, connect people, capture moments, and reflect changes. As we challenge the students in our classrooms to consider artifacts as representative of their own stories and of others, we create intertextual experiences that foster dialogue between students' lives, those of their classmates, and those represented in texts. These dialogical encounters support comprehension and understanding. The sharing of these experiences can also spark interest and understanding that motivate students to engage with texts in ways they might not otherwise. This building on and drawing from shared experiences is the focus of the next chapter.

References

Coombs, D., & Freeze, R. (2018). Lives on display: Examining artifacts of hope. *English Journal, 108*(2), 20–30.

Coulter, D. (2001). Reverse time capsule essay. *Teaching English in the Two-Year College, 28*(4), 421.

Douglass J., & Guthrie, J. (2008). Meaning is motivating: Classroom goal structures. In J. Guthrie (Ed.) *Engaging adolescents in reading* (pp. 17–32). Corwin.

Dowd, F. (1990). What's a jackdaw doing in our classroom? *Childhood Education*, *66*(4), 228–231.

Dulaney, M. (2012). Using a prop box to create emotional memory and creative play for teaching Shakespeare's Othello. *English Journal*, *102*(2), 37–43.

Ekwueme, C. Ekon, E., & Ezenwa-Nebife, D. (2015). The impact of hands-on approach on student academic performance in basic science and mathematics. *Higher Education Studies*, *5*(6), 47–51.

Gibb, R., & Guthrie, J. (2008). Meaning is motivating: Interest in reading: Potency of relevance. In J. Guthrie (Ed.) *Engaging adolescents in reading* (pp. 83–98). Corwin.

Guthrie, J., Wigfield, A., Humenick, N., Perencevich, K., Taboada, A., & Barbosa, P. (2006). Influence of stimulating tasks on reading motivation and comprehension. *The Journal of Educational Research*, *99*(4), 232–245.

Hannaford, C. (2007). *Smart moves: Why learning is not all in your head*. Great River Books.

Knecht, R. (2021). Middle graders in motion: Using middle-grade verse novels to navigate transition and identity. *The ALAN Review 49*(1), 68–80.

Kucirkova, N. (2024). The explanatory power of sensory reading for early childhood research: The role of hidden senses. *Contemporary Issues in Early Childhood*, *25*(1), 93–109.

Kurin, R. (2013). *The Smithsonian's history of America in 101 objects*. Penguin.

Lonberger, R., & Lonberger, W. (1995). Enhancing literacy skills with a time capsule. *Teaching Pre-k-8*, *25*(7), 52–53.

Lubar, S., & Kendrick, K. (n.d.). *Looking at artifacts, thinking about history. Smithsonian learning lab: Artifacts and analysis: A teacher's guide to interpreting objects and writing history*. https://smithsonianeducation.org/idealabs/ap/essays/looking.htm

Moore, D. W., & Onofrey, K. (2007). Fostering literate academic identities during the first days of school. In J. Lewis & G. Moorman (Eds.). *Adolescent literacy instruction: Policies and promising practices* (pp. 286–303). International Reading Association.

Pahl, K., & Roswell, J. (2010). *Artifactual literacies: Every object tells a story*. Teachers College Press.

Prince William Network. (1997). *To kill a mockingbird by Harper Lee: Then and now: A distance learning adventure. Oracle ThinkQuest*.

Rasinski, T. (2–6 May 1983). *Using Jackdaws to build background and interest for reading*. International Reading Association, Paper.

Renninger, K. Bachrach, J., & Hidi, S. (2019). Triggering and maintaining interest in early phases of interest development. *Learning, Culture and Social Interaction*, *23*, 1–17.

Ross, J. A. (1988). Controlling variables: A meta-analysis of training studies. *Review of Educational Research*, *58*(4), 405–437.

Rutherford, F. (1993). Hands-on: A means to an end. *Project 2061 Today*, 3. Retrieved January 13, 2024, from http://www.project2061.org/publications/2061Connections/archive.htm

Schiefele, U. (1999). Interest and learning from text. *Scientific Studies of Reading*, *3*(3), 257–279.

Sterbenz, C. (30 April 2014). An incredibly ambitious time capsule was sealed 75 years ago today—here's what's inside. *Business Insider*. https://www.businessinsider.com/westinghouse-time-capsule-2014-4. Accessed February 24, 2024.

Strickland, K. (2005). *What's after assessment? Follow-up instruction for phonics, fluency, and comprehension*. Heinemann.

Swan, E. (2003). *Concept-oriented reading instruction: Engaging classrooms, lifelong learners*. Guilford.

Yedinak, M. (n.d.). Designing museum exhibits for the Grapes of wrath: A multigenre project. *ReadWriteThink*. https://www.readwritethink.org/classroom-resources/lesson-plans/designing-museum-exhibits-grapes#ResourceTabs4

Zahorik, J. (1996). Elementary and secondary teachers' reports of how they make learning interesting. *Elementary School Journal*, *96*(5), 551–564.

3

Simulations

One warm March afternoon, just a few days shy of the first day of spring in Bryan, Texas, Abby Scoresby quietly took attendance as her 10th graders responded to a writer's notebook prompt at the start of class. While they wrote, Abby busied herself checking out copies of the book they were about to begin—Ray Bradbury's dystopian novel *Fahrenheit 451*.

But before the students finished writing, the principal entered the doorway—clipboard in hand—and motioned for Abby. In a quiet voice, but loud enough for the students to hear, he explained, "We just got something from TEA [Texas Education Agency] about a list of banned books. Every book that you teach—all of them—are banned."

Abby looked at him in disbelief. "All of them? *To Kill a Mockingbird? Othello? I Am Malala? Persepolis?*" She asked.

"All of them," the principal explained. "Starting tomorrow, you can't teach them—you can't even talk about them."

Abby just stared forward. "Even *Fahrenheit 451?* I need to come up with a whole new curriculum?"

The principal just shook his head. "I'm afraid so. I'm sorry," he replied and silently walked into the hallway.

The instant the door closed behind him, every head in the room turned towards Abby and the questions began to fly. "What just happened?!?"

"This is ridiculous!"

"You're telling me *Othello* got banned?"

"They don't want us to read *To Kill a Mockingbird*? Is it because it exposes racism?"

Abby couldn't respond to the inquiries coming at her from every angle.

"What's left for you to teach? Picture books?"

"They just don't want us to hear different opinions!"

"I normally don't like reading, but I actually liked the books this year. This is a huge bummer."

"Are you going to cry Mrs. Scoresby?"

Without Abby's prompting, some students brainstormed solutions, while others pulled out their Chromebooks, researching phrases like "Texas book bans." Still others started making plans to act. "We can fight this!" one student said. "My mom works at the district office. I'll see if she can figure this out," offered another. "Online it says the bans don't start until April 1st. Maybe we could read the whole book before then and the district would never know!"

After a few minutes, amid a flurry of scheming and discussion, Abby called the class to attention. "I need you to pause. Think about how you are feeling right now," she said. "Why are books important?" A few students offered perspectives and then Abby continued.

> We are still reading *Fahrenheit 451*. Although book bans are happening, what the principal said about our books right now isn't real. This was a simulation of a real experience, but not actually real. I wanted you to experience what it would feel like if it was against the law to read the books we've studied. This is important to think about as we begin our next novel.

The students sat in silence for a few seconds. "Wait, what?"

As most of the students processed what Abby said, she asked again: "How did you feel when you thought you couldn't read these books?"

After a minute of silence, students started to explain their responses. Abby listened until the bell rang and she reassured the class, "We will finish this discussion tomorrow."

This back-and-forth dialogue provides a glimpse into the simulation Abby orchestrated to acquaint her class with some of the conflicts and themes at the center of *Fahrenheit 451*. The term simulation comes from the Latin "similis," which means "like, resembling, of the same kind" or "simulare," meaning "to imitate." Aptly named, learning simulations take varying forms, but seek to imitate or create experiences that resemble real-life conflicts, struggles, or situations central to texts.

Although simulations are used regularly in courses such as history, business, and economics, this chapter considers simulations as powerful dialogical approaches for teaching literature and reading. When used in these contexts, simulations bring students, their feelings, and their lives into the heart of the inquiry by putting students into direct contact with the text's conflicts, settings, themes, and dilemmas.

What Makes Simulations Dialogic?

Literature itself provides a type of simulation as reading allows people to explore ideas, experiences, and events vicariously through words (Wolf, 2018). Unfamiliar people, places, and events become real as words on a page bring the reader into the life of the other. Similarly, simulated experiences bring texts to life as teachers turn abstract or potentially difficult concepts into stimulating tasks. These tasks engage readers' emotions, personalizing the material, and increasing comprehension.

Although teachers might take one of several approaches to simulations, effective simulations share five characteristics that make them dialogical. First, simulations support content-rich instruction anchored in themes, conflicts, or dilemmas within the text. Deep reading requires students to bring their background experiences into dialogue with words on the page. Every student comes to class with a unique background of rich and meaningful experiences, but sometimes they don't activate this knowledge and connect it to their reading. Simulations create immediate experiences that put students face-to-face with "replications of a real environment" where they encounter similar conflicts, themes, or struggles to those in the texts. These simulated experiences require them "to take action and make decisions as if they were actually operating in that environment" (Troyka & Nudelman, 1975, p. vi). In other words, the problem-posing nature of simulations puts students in real-time dialogue with the situations in the text and with each other. As students confront ambiguities, nuances, and uncertainties central to the text themselves, they become active participants in the inquiry.

Second, simulations provide intertextual experiences that engage students in stimulating tasks and trigger their interests in the conflicts, themes, and ideas in the text. Simulations require students to work out problems or develop solutions in contexts that simulate real emotions, perspectives, and feelings. Experience with these tasks triggers situational interest and then becomes background knowledge that students draw on during reading (Nolen & Nichols, 1994; Guthrie et al., 2006). As students explore solutions, consider implications, and reflect on their own responses through direct, lived experience, they exercise their agency to make decisions (Asal, 2005; Ellington et al., 1998). These experiences then become "texts" students use to make sense of their reading.

In addition, simulations motivate students to engage with readings at the heart of the inquiry. When used before reading, simulations entice students into the texts by engaging them in personal wrestles with issues and conflicts (Morton & Renzy, 1971; Mindich, 2000), typically by replicating or imitating historical circumstances or movements (Arnold, 1998; Muir, 1996), facilitating a personal experience with conflicts or themes (McCann, 1996), presenting ethical dilemmas (Wheeler, 2006), and debating these issues (Reimer & Brock, 1988). Engaging in these ways prior to reading improves comprehension (Smagorinsky et al., 1987) and increases retention (Shaw & Switky, 2018), ultimately helping both students and teachers achieve the cognitive and affective objectives of the reading (Arnold, 1998).

Third, simulations are, by their very nature, dialogical and require the consideration of multiple perspectives to explore a problem. Whole-class simulations require that students dialogue with their peers and teachers to explore questions, address conflicts, and work together to unpack dilemmas (Arnold, 1998). Students "grapple with tough issues, sometimes disagreeing, but in a civil and rational way, learning complex ways of communicating, and productive means of problem solving" (McCann et al., 2015, p. 5). They ask questions of one another, share their own understandings, and co-construct solutions as they consider multiple perspectives and interpretations of ideas. The questions inherent in the simulation spark inquiry and discussion as students wrestle with ideas, promoting interaction and collaboration (Shaw & Switky, 2018).

Simulations invite students to "try on" situations, feelings, and responses in the text. As students assume new roles and experience new situations in simulated contexts, they also experience the emotions that accompany them (Immordino-Yang & Faeth, 2010). These emotions help them better understand the perspective of the other and build empathy (Arnold, 1998; Johannessen, 1993). Experiencing the dilemmas and conflicts has also been shown to have a deeper and longer lasting impact than simply discussing the desired outcomes (Sanders, 2013).

The immersive nature of simulations also temporarily upends the academic playing field by putting students in situations where traditional social, academic, and environmental structures don't necessarily offer advantages (Guthrie et al., 2006). In this way, simulations create a common ground of experience for all learners through concrete, hands-on experiences that increase the accessibility of language and literacy demands for neurodiverse students (Dalton et al., 1997; Mastropieri et al., 1999) and create authentic purposes for reading, writing, speaking, and listening for all students (McCann et al., 2015).

Fourth, in addition to sparking discussion among learners, simulations require students to make arguments as they identify solutions to challenges and dilemmas posed. Preparing to participate in role play simulations cultivates critical reading skills among students as they read with an authentic purpose and through a specific lens (Stevens, 2014). In their preparations, students identify evidence, develop arguments, and consider rebuttals for their arguments. In addition, as students work through the conflicts presented in actual simulations, they employ argumentation and higher-order thinking skills that require going beyond the recall of facts and analyzing unfamiliar situations, weighing possible options, and synthesizing varied perspectives (Wheeler, 2006). The application of argument skills to an authentic context makes these skills relevant beyond the classroom and helps students draw connections to their own lives and experiences.

Finally, debriefing and reflection helps students not only summarize what happened in the simulation, but also provides opportunities for students to consider their feelings, behaviors, and beliefs and then evaluate their responses. During this time students share their personal reactions to the simulation, emotions they felt, and connections they made. Part of what makes simulations dialogical is their emphasis on students unpacking the experience through reflection and discussion. For this reason, teachers should avoid the temptation to explain what students should have gotten out of the experience and instead craft discussion questions that require students to discover the links between the simulation and real-world situations. These discussions help students better understand the connections between the simulation and its relation to the reading.

Reading simulates what it means to try on the lived experiences of others, including the emotions, struggles, and challenges of their lives. However, this type of empathy and experience can only take place in the reader when "feeling and thought" are connected in the reading circuit, and that thought "depends on the background knowledge and feelings" the reader brings to the reading experience.

> Words can only be understood when they provoke some kind of image in the mind of the learner. If students cannot access the underlying images, the words are not comprehensible...Experiences, on the other hand, are direct and real. They involve senses, emotions and movements,

and engage the learner fully. Real things happen when we experience with our senses, and in the experiencing we observe, relate to past experiences and notice patterns. Words are useful in this process, they help us to organize our thoughts about the sensations. But they are no substitute for the force and vividness of actual experience.

(Hannaford, 1995, p. 49)

In other words, language is essential to learning, but experience activates the senses and makes words come to life. Consider Travis's dilemma in Chapter 1 where he had no feelings for words. Simulations help call up feelings and experiences that can be used to put emotional and literal meaning behind words that imbue texts with meaning.

Applications and Examples of Simulations

Thus far I've used the term "simulation" generally to describe any variety of classroom activities that simulate or imitate real-life situations. But different types of and approaches to simulations exist that teachers should consider as they determine the appropriateness of simulations for their classes. The classroom examples that follow illustrate how immersive simulations, simulation games, role play simulations, and metaphorical simulations utilize these elements to provide dialogical experiences that spark discussion and bring the study of texts to life.

Immersive Simulations: Book Banning

This chapter began with a glimpse of the simulation Abby facilitated to help her students better understand book bans in the futuristic Midwest of the United States of Ray Bradbury's *Fahrenheit 451*. It would be easy to assume simulating book bans would be unnecessary because at the time book bans were at an all-time high across the United States—including in Texas, where Abby and her students lived. Wouldn't Abby's students experience actual book bans in their lives and communities? But the previous year, when stories of book banning made headlines across the nation, Abby had assigned *Fahrenheit 451* for summer reading and experienced an almost complete lack of engagement. In her own words, it went "terrible." None of the students seemed invested in reading the book. When Abby tried to lead a discussion about book banning, multiple students made comments like "Who cares if they burn some books? I don't even like reading."

Although her students the previous year did not see (or perhaps acknowledge) the similarity of the themes in the book and the world around them, Abby suspected that firsthand experience with the challenges at the heart of the novel might elicit a different reaction from this year's students (Morton & Renzy, 1971). And, although providing a pre-brief of the simulation with students often optimizes participation and metacognition, Abby guessed that waiting to reveal the simulation to the students until after it finished would maximize the emotional and cognitive impact of the experience. Based on their participation in the spontaneous discussion that ensued as well as on the content of and the ideas generated in that discussion, Abby's hunch proved correct.

In contrast to the previous year's discussion, the question "What did you feel when you thought you couldn't read these books?" piqued students' interests at the end of the first day. When they returned to class, most of her 10th graders were already talking about the simulation before the period began. "I figured it wasn't real," one said. But the situational interest was almost palpable. As the bell rang and the class settled down, Abby explained they would start by reflecting on the simulation from the day before. She launched the discussion by asking "What do we lose when we ban books?" Students began volunteering answers and words like "imagination," "history," "empathy," "understanding," "freedom," and "other perspectives" repeatedly emerged in their discussion about why society needs literature. As their study of the novel continued, these same themes came up in discussions as they considered the lives of the characters and their own.

Throughout the unit Abby noted a higher level of comprehension among the students. The quality of discussion increased, particularly the students' abilities to make connections between the themes, conflicts, and events in the book and their world.

For instance, before they even reached the end of Part One, students frequently described their distaste for Mildred. This became particularly true when Guy tried to talk to Mildred, but she was too deeply immersed in the story playing out on the TV-like parlor walls. When he asked her to turn them off, she refused because she valued the strangers on the screen like family.

Exasperated, Lamarcus explained, "Oh my gosh, it's so annoying when Guy was stressed and Mildred was so obsessed with screens, she wouldn't even talk to him." Abby paused and said, "That is frustrating. Maybe that's what it's like for your parents when you're on your phones?" The silence that followed seemed to provoke an epiphany on behalf of multiple students in the room. "Oh, maybe it is," he confessed with chagrin.

These and other connections students made throughout the unit engaged them in dialogue with one another, with the text, and with the implications of the ideas in their own lives. In contrast to students the previous year, their ultimate engagement in the text and its themes resulted in higher comprehension of the text itself and increased understanding.

Other Ideas for Immersive Simulations

The most famous immersive simulation may be the brown eyes, blue eyes experiment conducted in a 3rd grade classroom in Iowa in 1968. The teacher gave special treatment to the brown-eyed children one day, complimenting their outfits and behaviors, giving them extra privileges like extended recesses or privileged spots in lines, and conversely ridiculing and discriminating against the blue-eyed children (Bloom, 2005). The next day she reversed the roles and discriminated against the brown-eyed children and favored the blue-eyed children. This simulation proved a powerful learning opportunity for some, but controversy still rages around the ethics of this experience and the effect of this treatment on the development of young children. Consider this simulation in the 21st-century-setting of cell phones and social media, parental involvement, and diverse schools where so many already experience discrimination. In the current context, exercise caution with immersive simulations. When students don't realize they are participating in a simulation, taking the experience beyond the length of a class session can lead to unintended concern and fallout if the drama feels too real, especially if the simulation reinforces rather than challenges existing stereotypes and privilege.

However, despite these cautions, immersive simulations have a place in the curricula. Consider portraying the injustice of discrimination based on favorite sports teams or singers. What if the teacher gave "failing grades" on an assignment to all the students who cheer for the latest Super Bowl or NBA championship team or Taylor Swift fans just because the teacher disagrees with these tastes? Simulated discrimination based on these factors can also introduce the senseless but real discrimination characters endure, but without the real-life emotional and social implications. Consider texts like *The Grapes of Wrath, The Hate U Give, Dear Martin, The 57 Bus, The Way I Used to Be, American Born Chinese*, or other books that portray racist, sexist, homophobic, or other discriminating encounters and the ways characters wrestle with these experiences.

Teachers also use immersive simulations to introduce texts like *Lord of the Flies* and *The Hunger Games* that explore themes of social Darwinism, temporarily placing students in self-governing groups that write their own laws and then depend on one another for survival. Others pit student against student and demand selling out one's peers under cheating allegations for texts like *The Crucible* or to simulate reporting others to Big Brother in *1984* or the government in *I Must Betray You*.

Simulation Games: Who's the Witch?

Marion wanted to use a simulation to introduce Arthur Miller's play *The Crucible*. This play, set in the late 1600s in the Massachusetts Bay Colony, tells a dramatized version of the Salem Witch Trials that began with a group of teenage girls whose hysterics lead to accusations of witchcraft that eventually ripple throughout the entire community. She wanted to facilitate an experience less involved than an immersive simulation, but something that still helped students realize the impact of hysteria and groupthink. She selected a simulation game to provide this experience.

Simulation games involve students in an "overt competition of some sort" seeking to achieve an ultimate objective within a framework of rules or constraints that dictate the behaviors of the participants (Ellington et al., 1998, p. 1). In these games, the constraints created by rules typically feature aspects of reality, behaviors typical of human social interaction, or phenomena integral to the text as well as a clearly stated goal that defines what it takes to win (Brewbaker, 1972). For example, when Tom McCann (1996) taught *My Antonia*, he described how playing the game Oregon Trail allowed his students to better understand some of the challenges and perils pioneers faced. The game, with direct consequences for failing to survive (death) and clear expectations of what it takes to survive (win), simulated what the real pioneers faced on the trail.

It was late October in New Mexico when Marion's 11th graders began reading *The Crucible*. Earlier in the week they had read most of Act I, in which suspicions are heightened, and the accusations begin. Each day Marion started class with a roll call question—a question loosely connected to the content meant to get students talking. On this particular day, Marion asked students to look around the room and answer the following question: "Which classmate here do you trust the most?" Some students contemplated quietly while others glanced around nervously. As she called each student's name, they responded by naming another student in the class. A few laughed at their own answers and the class laughed when a student said an unexpected name or the name of someone other than the person who named them earlier—as when Joseph said Trenton's name, but Trenton named Javier instead of Joseph as his most trusted classmate.

Marion then asked the class to re-read the last page of Act I and after a brief discussion about the mood of this scene and the feelings it conjured in readers, she asked "Do you believe the accusations the girls are making?" Students shared a variety of responses, almost all agreeing that the girls seemed involved in some kind of witchcraft but split on whether they thought the girls might actually be real witches or possessed by evil spirits.

Marion then introduced the game "Who's the Witch?," a simulation that involved a conflict that mirrored the issue at the heart of the play, with the following instructions:

> Pretend, for a moment, that we are in Salem during the witch trials. It is rumored that at least five witches live amongst you (these witches know who they are). Your goal is to form a group of students that does NOT have a witch in it. At the end, any group that includes a witch fails this assignment. Pay attention to the evidence on each student's paper. Take notes about who you think is a witch and why—what did they do and does it make them a witch?

Marion then distributed papers that assigned students a witch or Puritan identity. Pulled from actual history, the play, and fiction, the slips included information such as "reads strange books at night," "goes for walks at twilight," "laughs during prayers," or "put a frog in a pot of boiling water" (see Figure 3.1). On the surface these accusations seemed harmless, but they mirrored "evidence" used in the play and in the real-life Salem trials to justify accusations of witchcraft.

Marion then announced the class had 15 minutes to determine the identities of the witches and form their groups. She also included a few important reminders: students put themselves at a disadvantage by sticking with their friends, so they shouldn't expect allegiance from anyone. She used the phrase, "This is all about doing what's best for you," more than once and emphasized friends may choose not to stick with friends.

The class immediately began talking, asking questions and self-selecting into groups. Initially, students gravitated toward their friends, but they soon realized they shouldn't trust everyone, and some accusations raised eyebrows. More than once students said things like, "You're kidding! You won't let me in your group?" in lighthearted disbelief as they tried to discern one another's true identities. Soon students who didn't typically talk to one another began engaging in discussion together. A few shy students stuck with their friends, a few identified as

FIGURE 3.1 "Who's the Witch?" identities

"obvious" witches stood alone, but the rest of the room filled with clusters of three to four students—some of whom trusted one another, and others who grouped together because no one else trusted them.

When the 15 minutes concluded, students returned to their seats. Marion announced, "All witches, please raise your hands." The room was quiet as students looked around, checking their accuracy against their list of accusers—but not one hand hung in the air. The class sat silent.

Finally, Marion confessed: no one had been assigned the role of "witch." Almost all students reacted, sharing comments like "Are you kidding me Miss?!?" or "I spent so much time figuring this out!" or "Oops, I guess I should have trusted him..." could be heard across the room. Although the discussions and condemnation remained lighthearted, the impact of the experience rippled throughout the classroom as students questioned their own judgment and certainty about their peers.

Once the class calmed down and felt reassured that they would receive full points for participating in the activity, they unpacked what happened. Marion asked them to respond in writing to the following questions:

- Why did friends turn their backs on friends?
- Against whom did you make judgments? Were they warranted?
- What emotions did you feel?
- Did you choose to join forces and unite in bigger groups or remain solo? Why?
- What were the benefits and drawbacks of secluding to protect yourself?

Before launching into a class discussion, Marion showed two short videos to build context and more awareness about mob mentality and mass hysteria, two of the conflicts they experienced in the simulation. After the videos, students reflected once more in writing, this time responding to the question: "What did the simulation and the information you learned about hysteria and mob mentality teach you?" (see Figure 3.2).

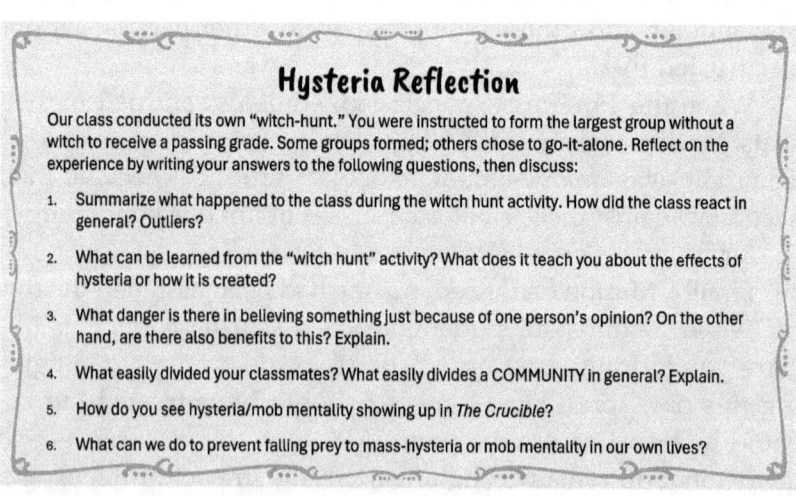

Hysteria Reflection

Our class conducted its own "witch-hunt." You were instructed to form the largest group without a witch to receive a passing grade. Some groups formed; others chose to go-it-alone. Reflect on the experience by writing your answers to the following questions, then discuss:

1. Summarize what happened to the class during the witch hunt activity. How did the class react in general? Outliers?
2. What can be learned from the "witch hunt" activity? What does it teach you about the effects of hysteria or how it is created?
3. What danger is there in believing something just because of one person's opinion? On the other hand, are there also benefits to this? Explain.
4. What easily divided your classmates? What easily divides a COMMUNITY in general? Explain.
5. How do you see hysteria/mob mentality showing up in *The Crucible*?
6. What can we do to prevent falling prey to mass-hysteria or mob mentality in our own lives?

FIGURE 3.2 Reflection questions and discussion points for debriefing about the "Who's the Witch?" simulation

Students wrote for 10 minutes and after they had finished, they participated in a tea party discussion where students stood up and walked around the room while music played. When the music stopped, they turned to someone near them and shared their reflections and writing. After each partner shared, they signed one another's papers and found another person to share with and discuss.

Although these reflections and discussions occurred at the conclusion of Act I, the impact of the simulation game could be felt throughout the rest of the unit. Throughout the reading of the play the class discussion often referred to parallels between the simulation and the text. For instance, at the end of Act III, where Abigail and the girls pretend to see a yellow bird attacking them, the class questioned whether the girls all wanted to lie or if mob mentality was to blame. As students shared different ideas and refenced the simulation, they remembered how easy it was to slip in groupthink, distrusting what they knew and going along with the crowd.

This same simulation could be used with young adult historical fiction about the Salem Witch Trials, including classics like *The Witch of Blackbird Pond, A Break with Charity: A Story about the Salem Witch Trials*, and more recent stories like *Fever, 1793*. Or it might also be adapted to the study of texts that highlight modern-day witch hunts. For example, the snuffing out of anti-German sentiments during World War I depicted in the YA novel *Sacred Shadow* or the anti-communist Red Scare in the years following World War II, seen in the historical fiction novel *Suspect Red* or the graphic novel *Red Scare*.

Other works, such as the YA novels *We Are Not Free, Beneath the Wide Silk Sky*, and the graphic novel *Displacement*, portray the imprisonment of Japanese Americans in internment camps during World War II. Also, the Lavender Scare targeted homosexuals in the 1960 through the 1990s, as seen in *Last Night at the Telegraph Club*. Or, even in the realm of fantasy or science fiction in books like *Scythe*, where corruption within the Scythdom and fear of standing up the Scythe Goddard lead to chaos. The study of these texts, as well as the fear and hysteria of the eras they portray, might all be enhanced through adaptations of the witch hunt simulation game.

Other games with different objectives might help readers consider conflicts or struggles at the center of a work. For example, a game like Beanboozled, which mixes chance with luck, can be used to simulate the impossible dilemma faced by the young man in Frank Stockton's short story "The Lady and the Tiger." Or the party game known as Mafia or Werewolf, which pits the uninformed majority against an informed minority, could be used to mirror the conflict in mystery novels such as *And Then There Were None* or *One of Us Is Lying*. This game could also work for books like Harry Potter that contain secret societies or books like *I Must Betray You, Fountains of Silence*, or any of the texts mentioned previously that feature past or present-day witch hunts.

Another simulation game, Lifeboat, places students on a sinking ship where only five of the nine passengers can fit on a lifeboat. Various forms of this activity are available online from educational, leadership, and religious organizations, such as Caritas Australia (2024) and Lenape Regional High School (n.d.). Regardless of the number or source, each involves making decisions about which passengers—based on vague initial descriptions—get a place in on the lifeboat. For example, four of the passengers include a teacher, a marine biologist, a chef, and a body builder. In the first round of the simulation each student picks five of the nine people to save and advocates for them based on why these people might be helpful to the group's survival.

But, as the next round begins, students learn more about each passenger's background and the situation shifts—the teacher is a smoker dying of lung cancer; the chef's restaurant was recently shut down because of sanitation issues; the marine biologist possesses an extensive knowledge of the sea; and the bodybuilder stowed away on the ship to evade an accusation of murder. The emerging details shift students' perspectives, quickly evolving into debates about the ethics and the value of a life. After each defends their choices to the group, the larger reflective discussion explores what factors shaped those decisions, the way society attributes worth, and how those valuations prove problematic. This game pairs nicely with *The Scarlet Letter, A Separate Peace, Pride and Prejudice, Monster, Speak, The Outsiders* and a myriad of other texts that grapple with the complexities of appearances and realities.

Role Play Simulations: The Draft

Last time JC taught Chris Crowe's YA novel in verse *Death Coming Up the Hill*, his students were captivated by the 976 haiku stanzas that came together to tell the story of Ashe, a high school senior wrestling with the everyday challenges of teenage life as the Vietnam War raged across the ocean and in his family. JC knew his current students would enjoy the book as well, but he also wondered how he might make the history and conflicts personal to 8th graders living in rural Idaho over 50 years later.

JC began the inquiry "Do individuals have a duty to others, their families, or their countries?" with a prop box exploration to focus their attention on significant symbols and themes in the book. He organized the class into small groups and gave each a prop. The students in the group had 90 seconds to answer the questions: "What is this? What does it make me think of? How do I think it might appear in the book?" Then they recorded their answers on their graphic organizers, passed the object to the next group, and picked up another—a tie dye shirt, a death notice, a Marine core "Sempre Fi" sticker, a draft card, a number 17, and hamburger. Once the groups finished rotating objects, each student used their predictions to write a paragraph describing what the book might be about, then shared those with the class.

The props ignited students' interests while helping them practice making inferences and unpacking the symbols in the novel. The novel's unique format also made it important for students to attend to vocabulary and word choice to comprehend major concepts and explicitly stated details as well as implied details. Specifically, what did words like "draft" and "deferment" mean to 13-year-olds in 2024 and how might JC help students develop a deeper understanding of these concepts?

JC decided to create a role play simulation to help students connect these unfamiliar words to concepts from the novel that held significant meaning. In role play simulations students take on assigned roles and then make choices or work through scenarios as if they were the people themselves (Monash University, 2024). As students face the scenarios and wrestle with challenges, they do so in a safe environment. Like the game simulation Marion facilitated with "Who's the Witch?" as they read *The Crucible*, students engaged as knowing participants in this role play with an awareness that the simulation was only a simulation.

Before the class began Chapter 4, JC started class by posing a question for students to respond to in their writer's notebooks: "Do you think people have a duty to serve their country in the military?" Students wrote for a few minutes, then began sharing their thoughts. After multiple students shared, JC explained that, in the US, men are required to register for Selective Service when they turn 18 and also observed how, during Vietnam, one-third of the men who fought—approximately 1.9 million—were drafted.

Then JC put a number on the Smartboard—97-0299496-4—and asked if any of the students could guess its significance. "Is it a social security number?" and "Is it an old-fashioned phone number?" were two guesses students ventured. After a few more, one student asked, "Wait—is it a draft number?" JC then explained it was a draft number and that the first two digits represented the person's birth year. "Do you know whose draft number this is?" JC asked. "It's mine."

JC explained that to better understand how the draft worked, the class would simulate the draft. He then distributed profiles to each male in the room, complete with a number between 1 and 15 as well as brief details about a man the number represented (see Figure 3.3).

For example, one read "I'm 21, I just graduated from trade school, and I am beginning my job as a plumber," and another "I'm a single father with three kids. The oldest is seven." A few others included "I have mild asthma, but I might be willing to shoot myself in the foot," "I am 23, I am almost done with college, but I might switch majors, just so I don't have to go to war," and another "I'm 19 and I'm a ski bum. My dad is a big-time lawyer for an international law firm."

Because the 1969 draft only included men, the females in the class received descriptions of draft exemptions and deferments to read to the class. These included words and phrases like college, dependency, family survivor, medical impairments, single parent, and religious student. JC also described options for

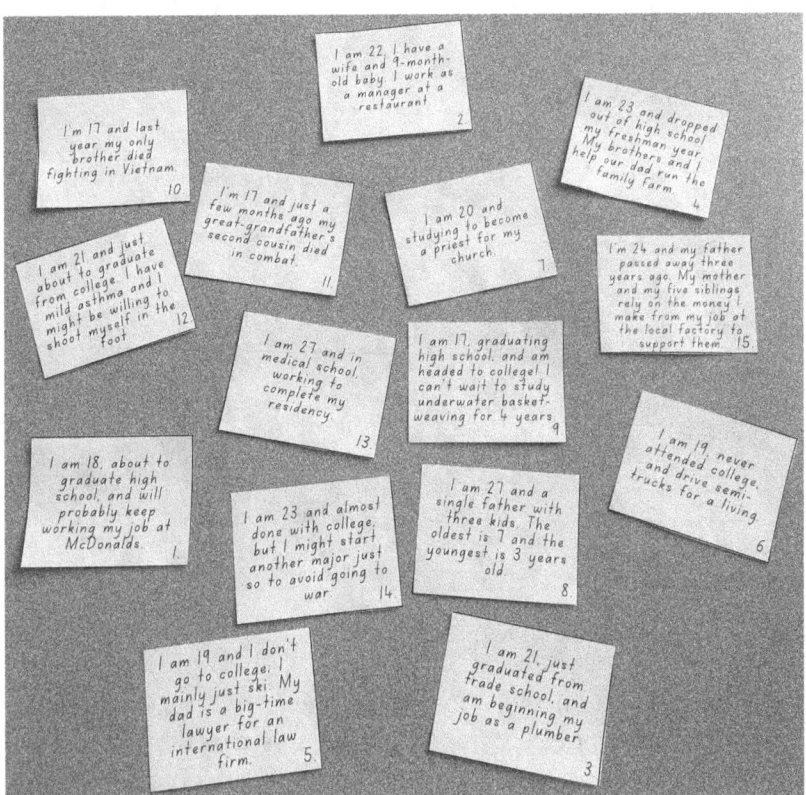

FIGURE 3.3 Draft profiles

escaping the draft, including refusal, fleeing the country, declaring noncombatant status, and becoming a conscientious objector.

With the profiles and exemptions distributed, the draft was ready to begin. JC stood in the back of the classroom with a basket containing the numbers. One by one he pulled out a number, and when each number was pulled, a boy took his place at the front of the room. Next, the class worked through the exemptions (See Figure 3.4).

As each girl read her exemption, any boy who thought the exception might apply to him would step forward and share his profile. For example, for the exemption "surviving family member," JC explained that some families had four or five male members drafted. In some cases, all those family members died, leaving the family devastated and without anyone to carry on

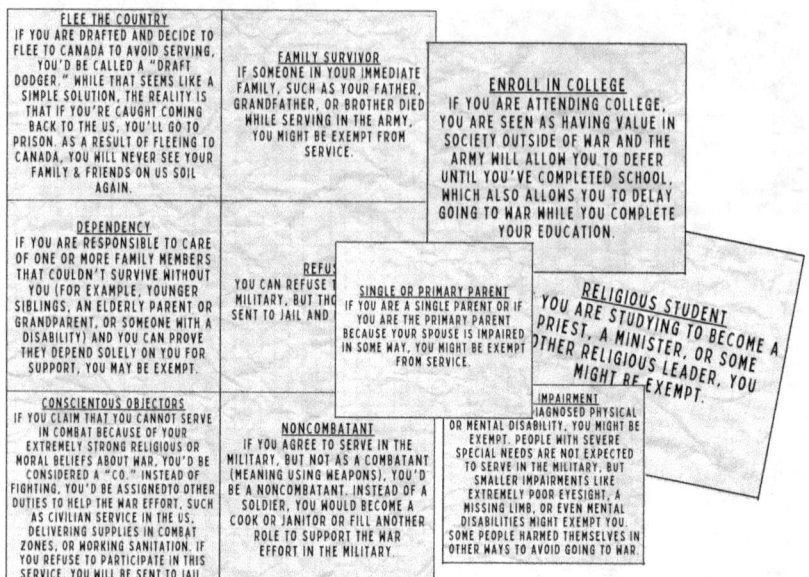

FIGURE 3.4 Draft exemptions

the family name. In those instances, the surviving male family member would not be drafted. When this exception was read a boy stood up and said, "That's me," then read his description that said, "My brother died fighting in Vietnam."

During the next 25 minutes of class, each exception was read, and the group of draftees were sorted. The boys watched one another become exempt until a handful of seats remained empty. As the students in the class observed the situation, they soberly considered the fate of each of their peers. Each exemption provided an opportunity to discuss why some people had more options than others when it came to draft dodging, deferment, and service. The students could see why some men served because their families needed the money—just like Ashe. JC used the word "poignant" as he recounted how the simulation provided 100% engagement and made them think deeply.

At the conclusion of the simulation, JC provided five questions to guide students' reflection on their experience. First, he asked students to go to a website called "1969 Vietnam War Draft Lottery." This website asked, "Would your draft number have been called?" and provided a brief explanation of how the 1969 draft worked and the way birth months and dates impacted which young men were drafted and which were not. Students entered their birthday, then wrote down their draft number and if it would have been called.

Next, they spent time responding in writing to these four questions:

1. Do you think the draft is fair? Why or why not?
2. Do you think that people have a duty to serve their country?
3. Is it fair that only men are required to register for the draft?
4. If you turned 18 and the US went to war, would you volunteer? If not, what would you do if you got drafted?

In the discussion that followed, students shared their responses and perspectives. Some questioned the equity of drafting women as well as men, while others complicated the gender issue by questioning whether the choice to only draft men resulted from the desire to protect women or because politicians thought less of women's abilities. Many of the boys unabashedly admitted they would not want to fight because of their fear of going to war. Afterwards, the class discussed their answers and made predictions about how the draft might impact the plot of the novel and the lives of the characters—particularly Ashe.

Although the draft simulation took place early in their reading of the novel, in the days that followed the simulation made the unfolding events more real and enhanced students' understanding. For example, the word "draft" is mentioned only seven times in the novel, but the haiku format offers little opportunity for context clues that provide background knowledge about what the draft was or how it worked. However, with the experience of the simulation, when the term "draft" appeared, it carried meaning and significance it had not previously possessed. Similarly, when soldiers or veterans of the war were mentioned, students better understood a piece of their experience. In these ways, simulations and experiential learning added meaning to the words and concepts students studied.

One moment occurred early in the novel when Ashe's mom gifted him a "Hell No, I Won't Go!" t-shirt while his father encouraged Ashe to join the college ROTC and then enlist as an officer. Other places included throughout the book when Ashe and his co-worker Rueben talked about Rueben's experiences serving in Vietnam, and at the end of the book at the bus depot when Ash was preparing to leave. The text did not directly state "Ashe is taking a bus to join the army so he can provide money to support his mom and baby sister," but it did contain details about heroes, love of family, and Angela sobbing as they say goodbye, swearing to keep his secret. Here JC stopped and asked students to use context clues to figure out what Ashe was doing and why he was going. As the students read and considered the possibilities, they thought back to the draft simulation, the exemptions, and why some people enlisted. "He's enlisting for the money! He's going to send it back to his mom."

Similarly, after the simulation and throughout the rest of the novel, JC noticed the students made repeated comments where they inserted themselves into the circumstances and situations Ashe faced. For example, in "Week 30," when Ashe contemplated Rueben's insights about how long the war might go on and whether college deferment would keep Ashe safe, some students said, "I'd just go to Canada!" or "I'd enlist as an officer." Or, when Ashe's dad met him for lunch and told him "You are going to be with me or against me," multiple students chimed in with comments like "I would definitely stand up to my dad," suggesting they saw themselves as Ashe and put themselves in his place.

Several historical fiction novels and nonfiction texts take place during the Vietnam era, making this simulation useful in other units of study. Memoirs like *The Things They Carried* and young adult nonfiction such as *Boots on the Ground: America's War in Vietnam*, *Captured: An American Prisoner of War in North Vietnam*, or *Courageous Women of the Vietnam War: Medics, Journalists, Survivors and More* offer compelling and heartbreaking insights into the complexities of war.

This specific simulation might also support the study of other young adult historical fiction that takes place during the Vietnam era, such as *Fallen Angels, The Wednesday Wars, Inside Out and Back Again,* or *All the Broken Pieces*. In addition, Larry Johannessen's book *Illumination Rounds: Teaching the Literature of the Vietnam War* offers ideas for other experiential learning opportunities, such as scenarios that explore heroism, simulations that mirror the perils of land mines and booby traps, as well as letters and oral histories that bring the voices of soldiers and civilians to life.

Novels with trial scenes also provide opportunities for students to participate in role play simulations. In these simulations different roles can be assigned that allow students to experience the ideological and moral wrestle that the characters face in the text. These role plays are not replications of the scenes, but instead students receive jury notices or summons to appear in court as characters are put on trial before the outcome in the text is revealed. Cases such as the ones in *12 Angry Men, To Kill a Mockingbird, Les Misérables, A Tale of Two Cities,* and *The Merchant of Venice* put students directly in the text. More contemporary texts like *Punching the Air* or *Monster* also center around court scenes. Even characters in texts that don't include court scenes can be put on trial—for example, trying Daisy for the death of Myrtle Wilson in *The Great Gatsby*. In this way, students engage in the moral reasoning required of the jury members and characters as they weigh decisions and options.

Metaphorical Simulations: Letters from Home

Kara's sixth year teaching brought with it a first-time opportunity: teaching 12th grade ELA. As she and a colleague considered which texts they wanted to include in their memoir unit and the needs of their students, *The Joy Luck Club* seemed like a perfect fit. The narrative vignettes that comprised the book invited reflection about themes of intergenerational sacrifice, family, culture, language, and the contrast between appearance and reality—more than a few ideas Kara knew would resonate with her students' lives.

In their school of almost 2600 students, half identified as Latinx, another 31% as white, and the rest of the school as Asian, Pacific Islander, African American, American Indian, or multiracial. Over half qualified for free/reduced lunch and several would be the first in their family to graduate from high school. Although most of the students had different racial and ethnic backgrounds from the characters in the novel, many of them experienced the tension the characters described, trying to dialogue between family or cultural expectations and their own goals. Kara and her colleague hoped reading the memoir-like text would invite students to reflect on their own experiences and inspire them to write about their lives.

Before beginning the book, the class participated in the lifeboat activity described earlier in the chapter, which led to deep conversations about people's inner and outer selves. These discussions paved the way for Kara's next activity where students completed an artifact-based inquiry—a paper bag collage where they thought about the tension between appearance and reality in their own lives. By identifying the differences and similarities between their inner selves and what external realities they presented, she hoped these two activities would prepare them to think about their own lives and experiences as they read the text.

To capitalize on this reflection Kara created a metaphorical simulation where students considered their lives "as if" they were characters from the novel. They had just finished reading selected vignettes as a whole class, including "The Joy Luck Club," "Two Kinds," "Double Face," and "Scar." As they prepared to read the next set of vignettes in jigsaw groups, Kara introduced an experience crafted to help students better understand what the characters in the novel were going through, particularly focusing on culture, family expectations, and intergenerational relationships. The goal of the metaphorical simulation was to investigate how the dreams, hopes, and realities the characters were influenced by their identities. She then introduced the "Letters from Home" assignment (see Figure 3.5).

Kara began by inviting students to think about a trusted adult in their lives. This person could be a parent, but it might also be any person the student felt a kinship or connection with, such as an older sibling, a neighbor, a church or community leader that knew the student, a grandparent, a coach, or a teacher that served as an example to them. She then explained that their homework

---

A LETTER TO YOUR STUDENT

Dear Wolverines:

In our class we've been reading *The Joy Luck Club* and examining the ways culture, family expectations, and intergenerational relationships shape the dreams, hopes, and realities of the lives of our characters. We've had some great discussions so far, but one way we can better understand literature is to link it to our own lives. So, I'm inviting you to have an experience that will help you relate to the characters.

Are you excited? I can almost hear you saying, "Oh, I can't wait! Where do I start?"

That's a great question...

FOR STUDENTS:
You will need to choose a trusted adult—a parent, grandparent, aunt/uncle, teacher, coach, mentor, church leader, older sibling, wise friend—to write YOU a letter.

FOR TRUSTED ADULTS:
You will be writing your student a letter. No, it will not be graded, BUT your student will be writing a response that *will be graded*. So PLEASE help them with this assignment!

You can choose to submit online through THIS LINK, or you can hand write them a letter, seal it in an envelope, and send it with them to school.

~~WHAT TO INCLUDE IN YOUR LETTER TO YOUR STUDENT~~

There is no word or page limit for your letter, but we do have a few things we'd like for you to include.

(1) What do you hope for your student in the future? What does an ideal future look like for your student?
(2) What things do you want them to achieve?
(3) What kind of person do you see them becoming? And what do you want them to continue doing to be that person?
(4) Is there something that you wish they would do differently? If so, why?
(5) What advice do you wish someone had given you when you were your student's age?

FIGURE 3.5 Letters from Home assignment sheet

was to ask this person to write a letter to the student about their hopes and dreams for the student's future. These might be things the adult wanted the student to achieve, the kind of person they hoped the student would become, or advice the adult wished they had received when they were at the same stage of life as the student. The adult could either submit the letter through an online link or send it to school with the student in an envelope, but the students could not read the letter before the assigned day in class.

As the class read through the assignment sheet together, Kara noted audible gasps and moans—some were bothered that they had to do another assignment, but most expressed excitement about the novelty of the project. Kara explained they had two weeks to submit their letters and over the next few days the letters began trickling in, both physically and electronically. Kara sent out email reminders to parents, notes home with students, and constant reminders to try and get maximum participation.

A few days later, after about 75% of the letters came in, Kara distributed the envelopes and the reflection assignment that accompanied it. The students who got letters opened them reading silently. Some cried. Kara explained,

> A lot of these kids complain about their parents all the time, but as they read their letters, they realized that teachers or adults who wrote letters really had their backs. The people who wrote the letters rose to the occasion and kids could definitely feel the love.

The students who didn't get letters were instructed to write a letter to themselves during this time and to think about their goals and aspirations for their futures. As they did so, Kara walked around and checked on them individually, offering encouragement and insights.

After the students finished reading their letters, Kara then introduced the other component of the experience—the reflection paper. In it, students described how the letter impacted them personally. She challenged students to think about the letter in terms of the cultural, familial, religious, or other factors. What resonated with them and where did they feel tension? What questions did it leave them wrestling with as they thought about their own futures? In their reflections, students also included at least one paragraph connecting their own experiences with something they read about in the novel. This might include words, experiences, or challenges faced by the characters. It could also include symbols they noticed in the book and in their own letter (see Figure 3.6).

Reflection on our Letter From Home

This assignment is what we call an "experiential reflection," or an analysis of a personal experience or observation. In your response, you will summarize and highlight underlying principles that support your analysis of the experience and make connections to *The Joy Luck Club*.

What does a reflection paper consist of?
The format of a reflection paper consists of three parts. These are:
- The introduction – this is where you will state your subject of reflection and thesis/main idea.
- The body paragraphs – this is where you will describe your experience, including your thoughts, feelings, and how the letter has affected you. You need to have at least ONE paragraph connecting your experience to things we have read in *The Joy Luck Club*.
- The conclusion – this is where you will summarize what you have found out, bringing your ideas and opinions together to restate your original thesis/main idea.

Use these sentence stems to help you write reflectively. This should be done in the first person. Remember, we are writing about how we FELT about the experience, not just the experience itself.

The most important thing was..	Later I realized…
I felt like…	This made me think about…
After thinking about it…	I wonder what would happen if…
I learned that…	A symbol that I'd like to create from this letter is…
I want to know more about…	My next steps might be to…
What I wish I could say back is…	I feel like my trusted adult does/doesn't the real me, and that makes me think…
I connect with (character) in *The Joy Luck Club* because…	My experience/relationship with my adult is similar/different to the characters in *The Joy Luck Club* because…

Here are some questions to consider when you write your reflection:
1. How has the letter affected me?
2. What have I learned?
3. Does the reading, lecture, or experience challenge you socially, culturally, emotionally, or theologically? If so, where and how? Why does it bother you or catch your attention?
4. Does the letter and experience leave you with any questions? Were these questions ones you had previously or ones you developed only after finishing?
5. Can you relate anything in your letter, either words on the paper or the experience you are having, to that of the characters in our book *The Joy Luck Club*? What character do you connect with most?
6. In thinking about symbolism in the book, what symbols do you see in your own letter? If there aren't any, can you come up with a symbol for yourself that would represent this experience?

FIGURE 3.6 Letters from Home reflection

After the letter experience, Kara offered students a list of the vignettes from the book and encouraged them to choose a vignette that resonated with their own experiences, particularly if the events, characters, and conflicts tied back to their letters. Students read their selected the vignettes in their jigsaw groups and as she monitored the chatter at different tables in the classroom, the soundbites she heard seemed to consistently involve dialogue about the letters and what was happening in the book.

The impact of this experience reached beyond just the discussion of the vignettes that day. Throughout the rest of their reading and studying of the novel, Kara noted more responsive reactions to the book. As the class continued to work through the text, students offered insights that reflected their personal understandings of the themes, conflicts, and ideas. They also made text-to-self connections more readily than in previous units, often beginning comments in class with phrases like "Remember that letter thing we did…" and then describing the connection they drew or "This thing in the book reminds me of that letter thing we did…" or even "So-and-so's mom said this…" and then relating it to something a character experienced in the text.

After they concluded their reading of the novel, the students each wrote a "This I Believe" essay, drawing on their notes and assignments throughout the quarter, including their letters and reflections. Kara could see the impact of the letter assignment as she surveyed the topics of the papers, noting that a few wrote about the importance of telling people how you feel, reaching out to adults who care, and even the value of writing letters. Other students selected a value or belief highlighted in their letters by a parent or noted adult and expounded on their own belief in that value.

Metaphorical simulations like the letter-writing experience could also be used with *Romeo and Juliet* or poems like "Those Winter Sundays" by Robert Hayden that reflect the nuances of intergenerational relationships. Other contemporary texts might include *American Born Chinese, The Poet X, Barefoot Dreams of Petra Luna, Esperanza Rising, We Were Liars, All My Rage, I Am Not Your Perfect Mexican Daughter, Long Way Down* or *House of the Scorpion*. Each of these novels explores the challenges teens face navigating the complexities of their intersecting and sometimes seemingly incongruous identities.

Beyond letter writing as described here, a variety of other metaphorical simulations allow students to experience parallels between the conflicts in texts and real life. For instance, the "Insider or Outsider?" experiment requires students to intentionally situate themselves as an outsider to social norms to temporarily simulate the discomfort and social angst that sometimes results from being on the outside of a group, culture, or society (Coombs & Mayans, 2015). Although not a replication of the real challenges faced by the characters in these novels, this metaphorical simulation might pair well with texts such as *The Perks of Being a Wallflower, Wonder, The Beginning of Everything, Mexican WhiteBoy, Openly Straight, All the Bright Places It's Kind of a Funny Story*, or *Starfish*.

Considerations

Simulations offer participants opportunities to participate in hands-on experiences that exemplify conflicts, themes, and dilemmas within texts, but within safe environments where learners can take risks and wrestle with ideas without experiencing real-world consequences (Lateef, 2010). Simulations also provide students with chances to "experience feelings of failure, rejection, poverty, excessive pressure, futility, hopelessness, and helplessness in a controlled simulation rather than in the real situation" (Kachaturoff, 1978, p. 222).

As teachers consider a simulation to initiate dialogue around an inquiry, they should begin by identifying what they want students to experience that will ultimately support the learning related to the text. For example, what dilemmas or questions would appear on an anticipation guide for the inquiry? What bigger questions might lend themselves to something more experiential and stimulate thinking about big questions in a deeper way?

Next, think about what kinds of activities might help provide this experience. A game? A role play? A metaphorical experience or an immersive simulation? McCann et al. (2015) recommended considering the environment for the simulation, any identities that students will form or assume, the central problems and conflicts, and information that will or will not be provided. Then, what questions or approaches need to be central to the reflection and debriefing experience so students can see the connections between the simulation and the text?

Remember that the rule "the simpler, the better" often applies to simulations. Don't give in to temptations to create big and complex events that perfectly mirror historical or plot events. Over-attention to extensive parallels often eclipses the experience and focus. In other words, sometimes less is more. Keep focused on the goal and at different points in the design process self-reflect by asking: is this still accomplishing the initial goal?

Approach the brainstorming and design of simulations as dialogically as students should—that is, in dialogue with co-workers and trusted colleagues who will provide perspectives and possible what-ifs that need to be considered. Talk through anticipated outcomes and allow the other person to play devil's advocate as you think through alternative scenarios. Consider modifications to the experience that might help reduce challenges or concerns. Make administrators a part of the dialogue as well. Their perspective can help troubleshoot challenges or open possibilities previously unconsidered.

Of all the dialogical strategies featured in this book, simulations should be approached and implemented with the most thoughtful awareness. It's almost impossible to appropriately "level" simulated experiences because their effectiveness and appropriateness depend on the context of the class and the developmental readiness of students (Ellington et al., 1998). What might be developmentally appropriate in one context with a particular grade might be too much for students in the same grade in another context. For this reason, it's also important to monitor simulations moment-to-moment as they unfold in the classroom. If a situation starts to get out of hand, intervene or pause the simulation.

Although implementing simulations requires teachers to navigate precautions, simulations are an effective tool to spark inquiry and dialogue. They harness the power of emotion and sensory experience to give students a taste of the situations, dilemmas, and conflicts represented in texts. It's this emotional engagement and the harnessing of social interactions in the process of learning that simulations—and our next strategy—provide.

References

Arnold, T. (1998). Make your history class hop with excitement (at least once a semester): Designing and using classroom simulations. *The History Teacher, 31*(2), 193–203.

Asal, V. (2005). Playing games with international relations. *International Studies Perspectives, 6*(3), 359–373.

Bloom, S. (2005 September). Lessons of a lifetime. *Smithsonian Magazine.* https://www.smithsonianmag.com/science-nature/lesson-of-a-lifetime-72754306/

Brewbaker, J. (1972). Simulation games and the English teacher. *The English Journal, 61*(1). 101–109, 112.

Caritas Australia. (2024). *Lifeboat activity*. Caritas Australia. Retrieved May 6, 2024 https://www.caritas.org.au/media/yyyajwph/the-lifeboat-activity.pdf

Coombs, D., & Mayans, M. (2015). Insider or outsider? Using young adult literature and experiential learning to understand the other. *The ALAN Review, 43*(1), 45–55.

Dalton, B., Morocco, C., Tivnan, T., & Mead, P. (1997). Supported inquiry science: Teaching for conceptual change in urban and suburban science classrooms. *Journal of Learning Disabilities, 30*(6), 670–684.

Ellington, H., Gordon, M., & Fowlie, J. (1998). *Using games & simulations in the classroom*. Kogan Page.

Guthrie, J., Wigfield, A., Humenick, N., Perencevich, K., Taboada, A., & Barbosa, P. (2006). Influence of stimulating tasks on reading motivation and comprehension. *The Journal of Educational Research, 99*(4), 232–245.

Hannaford, C. (1995). *Smart moves: Why learning is not all in your head.* Great Ocean Publishers.

Immordino-Yang, M. H., & Faeth, M. (2010). The role of emotion and skilled intuition in learning. In D. A. Sousa (Ed.), *Mind brain and education* (pp. 69–84). Solution Tree Press.

Johannessen, L. (1993). *Illumination rounds: Teaching the literature of the Vietnam War*. NCTE.

Kachaturoff, G. (1978). Learning through simulation. *Social Studies, 69*(5), 222–226.

Lateef, F. (2010). Simulation-based learning: Just like the real thing. *Journal Emergencies, Trauma, and Shock, 3*(4), 348–352.

Lenape Regional High School. (n.d.). *The lifeboat* Lenape Regional High School. Retrieved May 4, 2024 https://www.lrhsd.org/cms/lib05/NJ01000316/Centricity/Domain/842/The%20Lifeboat%20Activity.docx

Mastropieri, M., Scruggs, T., & Magnusen, M. (1999). Activity-oriented science instruction for students with disabilities. *Learning Disability Quarterly*, *22*(4), 240–249.

McCann, T. (1996). A pioneer simulation for writing and for the study of literature. *The English Journal*, *85*(3), 62–67.

McCann, T., D'Angelo, R., Galas, N., & Greska, M. (2015). *Literacy and history in action: Immersive approaches to disciplinary thinking, grades 5-12*. Teachers College Press.

Mindich, D. (2000). The Ada Valley simulation: Exploring the nature of conflict. *The English Journal 89*(5), 128–133.

Monash University. (2024). Role play/simulation. *Learning and teaching: Teach HQ*. https://www.monash.edu/learning-teaching/TeachHQ/Teaching-practices/Active-learning/active-learning/design-active-learning/active-learning-activities/role-play-simulation

Morton, J., & Renzy, R. (1971). Some teaching techniques for high school economics. *Journal of Economic Education*, *3*(1), 11–16.

Muir, S. (1996). Simulations for elementary and primary school social studies: An annotated bibliography. *Simulation Gaming*, *27*(41), 41–73.

Nolen, S. B., & Nichols, J. G. (1994). A place to begin (again) in research on student motivation: Teachers' beliefs. *Teaching and Teacher Education*, *10*(1), 57–69.

Reimer, C., & Brock, M. (1988). Books, students, censorship: Reality in the classroom. *English Journal*, *77*(7), 69–71.

Sanders, M. J. (2013). The university as a setting for experiential learning: The potential for reciprocal benefits. *Proceedings of the Human Factors and Ergonomics Society Annual Meeting*, *57*(1), 1590–1594.

Shaw, C., & Switky, B (2018). Designing and using simulations in the international relations classroom. *Journal of Political Science Education*, *14*(4), 523–534.

Smagorinsky, P., McCann, T., & Kern, S. (1987). *Explorations: Introductory activities for literature and composition, 7–12*. ERIC/NCTE.

Stevens, R. (2014). Role play and student engagement: Reflections from the classroom. *Teaching in Higher Education*, *20*(5), 481–492.

Troyka, L., & Nudelman, J. (1975). *Taking action: Writing, reading, speaking, and listening through simulation games*. Prentice-Hall.

Wheeler, S. (2006). Role-playing games and simulations for international issues courses. *Journal of Political Science Education, 2*(3), 331–347.

Wolf, M. (2018). *Reader, come home: The reading brain in a digital world*. Harper.

4

Drama

Although it was already an overcast, rainy October day outside of Madison's 8th grade classroom in Vancouver, Washington, she dimmed the lights for effect. Today's lesson served as the introductory piece to their exploration of suspense and horror in texts and their own lives. She pressed play, and the narrator began reading the first lines of Kelly Deschler's poem "The Hollow," inspired by Ichabod Crane's late-night ride in Washington Irving's iconic short story "The Legend of Sleepy Hollow." The speaker clearly but carefully read each line, giving voice to the rich imagery describing the haunted wood on that cold, dark October night. The sound of a breeze rustled through the trees and night songs of owls, ravens, and crickets reverberated faintly in the background.

But the forest noises didn't come from the recording. Adolescent fists stuffed into Red Solo cups generated the clippity clop of horses' hooves. Quiet whistles from a handful of students scattered across the room mimicked the whisper of the wind. Crumpled paper crunched like dry, dead leaves on the forest floor. The narrator's voice carried a certain steady but curious quality as the sounds accented their descent into the wood. The voice continued reading rhythmically, taking the listeners over a covered bridge as the full harvest moon shone in the black night, lighting the way through the twists and turns of the forest path.

Suddenly, at the mention of a wolf's cry, an "Owooooo!" interrupted the narration. The class erupted in laughter as they looked up and saw Joseph standing on his chair, howling at the Moon. Fully leaning into his task, Joseph took his assignment to create a wolf's cry seriously. Dramatic? Yes. A little over the top? To be sure. Madison paused, raised her eyebrows, and gently reminded the class "Stay focused!" But her grin also signaled her appreciation for Joseph's investment in the soundscape experience.

Earlier in the day, when Madison introduced the assignment, students wondered if what their teacher was asking was too good to be true. "You want us to make weird sounds?" one student asked in disbelief. "Not weird sounds," she clarified. "Sounds that appear in the poem. You're going to identify the sounds and then analyze how they build suspense and anticipation in the poem." As the class received their assignments, then brainstormed, planned, and coordinated in their pairs or small groups, almost everyone responded enthusiastically—those who typically performed well and those who sometimes struggled with engagement.

The soundscape crafted by Madison's class created a dialogical reading experience that engaged students in literary analysis and utilized the senses to transport them into the world of the text. The classroom examples in this chapter highlight the dialogic power of dramatic strategies to facilitate deep reading that increases comprehension, explores alternative perspectives, and cultivates empathy. Strategies like soundscapes, reader's theater, tableaus, and performing character approaches help teachers and students dialogue with texts, the world, and one another as they co-construct meaning.

What Makes Drama Dialogic?

Whether contemplating characters, reimagining a scene, or exploring imagery, dramatic strategies help students enter into dialogue with the other, exploring and experiencing the emotions, experiences, and understandings necessary to comprehend and deeply read texts. In fact, Louise Rosenblatt (1978) likened the transaction that occurs between a reader and a text to that of an actor preparing to perform his own interpretation of a text. She explained,

> We accept the fact that the actor infuses his own voice, his own body, his own gestures—in short his own interpretation—into the words of the text. Is he not simply carrying to its ultimate manifestation what each of us as readers of the text must do…?
>
> (p. 13)

In other words, in both drama and reading, people make sense of words by drawing on their own understandings, emotions, bodily experiences and abilities, memories, and feelings to bring characters, conflicts, and events to life.

However, the often-solitary, usually quiet act of reading allows some readers to passively decode words without transacting with their meaning and without really drawing on these personal, sensory elements. In contrast, the active, hands-on, and even dialogic nature of drama requires readers to slow down, to weigh the words on the page, re-enter the text, and consider the way these elements come into play. These types of connections foster deep reading that accesses the senses and draws readers into the text. For this reason, dramatic strategies serve as powerful tools for facilitating deep, dialogical reading experiences in the classroom.

First, content-rich instruction brings reading comprehension instruction into dialogue with the content students are learning, particularly through authentic inquiry and hands-on experiences. Dialogical strategies that involve drama and role play engage students in talking-to-learn activities that help them recall central ideas and plot details, as well as infer character's motivations, interpret relationship nuances, and analyze tone (Juzwik et al., 2013). When students who read superficially create enactments of literature, these strategies force them to read on a deeper level. As Douglass and Guthrie (2008) explained,

> By composing and practicing the parts, they read between the lines, imagine the characters' feelings, and link the

portion to prior sections. In short, knowing they have to act it out motivates them to deeply understand it. When this understanding dawns on students, their interest grows. As the text makes sense, they move forward with more confidence an eagerness.

(p. 23)

When students act out literature, they engage with the text more deeply because the nature of the task creates a need to understand it better. And, when they understand the text, they become more confident in their reading abilities and understandings of the text as well as more interested in the text and tasks themselves.

Second, dramatic strategies also facilitate intertextual approaches to comprehension through the inclusion of other texts, particularly students' own and others' experiences. Jeffery Wilhelm, a teacher researcher and advocate of drama in the classroom, explained that students who struggle with reading tend to read with less accuracy and proficiency than strong readers. They also tend not to draw on their background knowledge or "intertextual information," which includes the construction of texts, background knowledge, questions, interests, and other details important to discovering meaning in texts (Wilhelm, 1997/2008, p. 91). Enactment strategies require students to engage with this intertextual information—both their own and that of other students—as they construct meaning to bring the text to life. The hands-on, active nature of dramatic interpretation leads students to elevated comprehension.

Third, like simulations, dramatic strategies facilitate the understanding of multiple perspectives, requiring students to step outside of their own experience and consider the viewpoint of others. As students draw on evidence from the text to identify and try to understand someone else's perspectives and experiences, their own understandings of the world expand. Brian Edmiston (2014), a teacher and researcher of dramatic pedagogies, explained,

> Playing, like reading, is never completely losing yourself in another world but rather actively and intentionally creating an alternative reality where you can *experience*

> the world *as if* you were other people. Playing is choosing words and deeds to play with possibilities, trying out ways of acting in and on the world.
>
> (p. 14)

Reading and drama provide a vicarious experience that allows readers to enter into the emotional world of the other and consider perspectives outside their own, ultimately expanding readers' horizons. Experiencing conflicts and dilemmas "as if" they were another person helps students explore and consider possibilities they might not otherwise. This type of deep reading not only engages readers; it builds empathy as readers consider perspectives different from their own.

Finally, perhaps more than any of the other strategies discussed in this book, dramatic strategies require students to use evidence to support their interpretations. As students attempt to recreate texts and enact scenes, they form arguments to explain *how* and *why* details support their interpretation. Then, when these interpretations are made public—as typically happens when drama is performed—readers must also use evidence to support and sometimes even defend their interpretations and recreations of the text.

Applications and Examples of Dramatic Inquiries

At the beginning of this chapter, I described a portion of the soundscape that Madison's students performed as they studied "The Hollow." Creating a soundscape required students to read the text, then return to the text to identify sensory experiences within the poem. By mimicking the noises described or alluded to in the poem, students immersed themselves in the text and created a mood that shaped their interpretations. This use of drama—as well as the other uses described in this chapter—invite students to enter the text from the inside. Or, as Maryanne Wolf (2018) explained,

> Drama makes more visible what each of us does when we pass over in our deepest, most immersive forms of

reading. We welcome the Other as a guest within ourselves, and sometimes we become Other. For a moment in time we leave ourselves; and when we return, sometimes expanded and strengthened, we are changed both intellectually and emotionally.

(p. 44)

This immersion in the text helped readers activate their emotions and their minds. Both types of engagement are central to motivating students to read and find meaning within the story. The examples in this chapter demonstrate how soundscapes, reader's theater, tableaus, and performing character strategies increased student comprehension and engagement with texts before, during and after reading experiences (see Table 4.1).

TABLE 4.1 Dramatic strategies

Dramatic strategy	*Before, during, & after reading applications*
Soundscapes Students use their voices, hands, and props to create sounds on their own and with their peers that help convey the mood or tone of a text	**After:** After an initial reading of the text, students return to the text and identify sights, sounds, and other sensory components within an assigned portion of the chapter, poem, or scene. Identifying and creating these sounds gives them a purpose to revisit the text, to consider the context, and to engage in analysis.
Reader's theater Students receive a scripted version of a story or chapter and read the part of one of the characters or the narrator, using facial cues, sounds, gestures, and voice inflections to convey meaning	**Before:** Participating in a reader's theater presentation of a story before reading and studying the actual text can help students become familiar with the plot, characters, and conflicts of a story. This will help scaffold their understanding of the actual text as they wrestle with language and other ideas. **During:** The reading and re-reading required in reader's theater helps increase students' reading comprehension and reading fluency. **After:** Students can create their own reader's theater scripts that extend the story, present the story from the perspective of another character, or showcase deleted scenes from the text. Students can also synthesize sources and present their own reader's theater to tell a story they learned through independent reading and research.

(*Continued*)

TABLE 4.1 (Continued)

Dramatic strategy	Before, during, & after reading applications
Tableau Students work in small groups to position themselves in different poses that ultimately create a three-dimensional visual of an image or scene from the text	**During**: This strategy can be particularly useful for helping students do a close reading of a chapter or portion of text and drawing their attention to details that shape the narrative. Returning to the text to read or re-read details supports students' comprehension and informs the way they set up the scene. **After**: When used after reading, tableaus require students to summarize the text and identify pivotal moments of the narrative or story arc. If students are asked to brainstorm possible scenes to represent, it also helps them develop argument skills and practice using evidence to support their choices.
Conversations with Strangers Students work with partners to describe characters or recount scenes from a text as if they were telling the details from the perspective of another character in the text	**During**: As students learn more about different characters, this strategy helps them attend to different elements of characterization, consider the details that are and are not included in the narrative, and better understand voice. **After**: This strategy could be used as a review strategy to reinforce students' understanding of the narrative and to help students prepare for assessments focused on character analysis and point of view.
Good Angel, Bad Angel Hotseat One student represents a character in the text at a hinge point of a major decision; the other students in the class consider alternatives and advocate for different choices, presenting different perspectives and rationales for the choice	**Before**: Present students with dilemmas or "what if" situations that mirror those in the narrative and ask students to consider how they might respond to these conflicts. Then, as they read, they can identify parallels between their own responses and reactions and those of the characters. **During**: Use this strategy during reading to evaluate and consider choices characters might make and how the consequences of those choices shape the evolving narrative. **After**: Invite the students to assume their roles again, but instead of advocating for a particular position, ask them to consider their positions in hindsight and to defend their choices with evidence from the narrative.

(Continued)

TABLE 4.1 (Continued)

Dramatic strategy	Before, during, & after reading applications
Conscience Alley At a hinge point of a major decision in the text, students consider the character's options and decide which choice they will advocate for, making an argument for their perspective or drawing quotes from the text to support their position; one student represents that character and listens to or engages with their classmates' various perspectives as they walk between them	**Before**: Activate prior knowledge by presenting students with a scenario describing a dilemma faced by one of the characters in the text and ask them how they would respond. As students begin reading, they can consider their responses and note changes in their own and their peers' recommendations when considered from the perspectives of the characters within the text. **During**: This strategy is most often used during reading, before a character makes a major decision. It helps students thoughtfully consider the alternatives the character faces and the consequences for their decisions. **After**: To help students reflect on the consequences of decisions made by characters in the text, invite them to make a list of choices and outcomes characters could have made and hypothesize about how those choices would have led to different outcomes.
Character lines & tone Students receive a description of a character and practice reading and performing lines as if they were the character to better understand their dispositions, motivations, and behaviors	**Before**: Use this strategy to introduce attributes of characters like their voice, tone, values, and mood. Frontloading these kinds of key details can help students better understand the role each plays in the narrative and the relationships among characters. It can also be used to make predictions about characters. **During**: An extension and additional scaffolding to help students comprehend key chapters or sections would include giving students lines or quotes from the character that will appear in the text and asking them to try reading these lines the way their character would say them.

Soundscapes

Before Madison selected soundscapes as a strategy to support student engagement and literary analysis of the poem "The Hollow," she knew one thing: the previous year her students struggled to understand and analyze imagery. For this reason, she had intentionally chosen this poem, full of sounds, smells, and images that conveyed the suspenseful mood of the forest and tone characteristic of horrific literature. But she still needed a strategy to help students understand the effects of these details as they analyzed the poem.

Soundscapes breathe life into texts as students generate "a series of sounds (using voices without words, hands, several voices speaking together, repetitions, and echoes)" that come together to reflect the atmosphere or mood of a scene (DeBlase, 2005, p. 31). Creating soundscapes requires students to attend to the details within a text that describe the sights, sounds, and other sensory components within a chapter, poem, or scene. Soundscapes also help students visualize scenes as they interpret the details significant to the text. When Madison considered her goals for this lesson, a soundscape seemed like a natural fit.

To prepare students for the soundscape, Madison taught a minilesson on lyric poetry, characterized by its personal viewpoint, rhythmic pattern, and use of sensory language. They explored rhyme schemes and then read "The Hollow," labeling its ABAB CDCD pattern and discussing the rhythm created by the repeated rhyming sounds. Their discussion then shifted to sensory imagery. Madison challenged students to imagine a late October night and to ask themselves: What do you see? Hear? Smell? What might you touch? How might you feel on a night like this? Students brainstormed answers to each question, noting ways each sense contributed to the atmosphere. Then she introduced the soundscape.

After explaining how soundscapes work, Madison separated the students into small, predetermined groups of 2-3, each tasked with creating the sounds for two lines from the poem. Madison intentionally differentiated the tasks according to the abilities of the learners and their learning preferences. For example, she assigned students who struggled with comprehension lines containing clear examples of sound imagery. Students who already mastered the fundamentals of sensory imagery received lines that required making inferences to determine appropriate sounds. A mobility-impaired student who used a Tobii Dynavox eye-tracking system to communicate searched her sound database to identify files that might correspond with their assigned lines.

Quieter students who nervously participated in class still received line assignments, but they were paired with peers who helped them feel comfortable participating in dramatic recreations of the text.

After a few minutes of brainstorming and practicing, the class felt ready to perform their soundscape. Madison pressed "play" on the audio and the narrator read what had become familiar, rhythmic lines. Like an orchestra conductor, Madison led the students in the use of their voices, bodies, and a few props to replicate the sounds they identified in the poem. First came Reagan and Avery's Red Solo cup hoofbeats. Then Reese softly hooting like an owl. The whistle of Ezra's wind through the crumpling of paper leaves. Luke's dramatic howl. The croak of a bullfrog on Brielle's sound machine. Boyd offering his best caw of a crow. Finley and Grayson closing with their own hoofbeats, faster and more powerful than the earlier ones, but fading as quickly as they came. The class made small tweaks and then performed their soundscape again, masterfully orchestrating their parts so each voice contributed to the grand finale performance.

Identifying the sound imagery and creating it to emphasize the mood and tone of the scene offered an active, engaged way to get students participating in the reading experience. By the end of the day, across all five sections of her classes, over 65% of students indicated they felt the most confident in their abilities to analyze imagery, with another 30% feeling most sure about their ability to analyze rhyme. And over 80% of the students—including a handful who typically disliked everything—said they actually enjoyed the soundscape experience and that it helped them better understand imagery.

But the real test came the following day when Madison added the analysis component. She gave students copies of the poem and asked them to mark the imagery using different colored highlighters—yellow for visual imagery, pink for auditory imagery, and blue for olfactory imagery. They also answered analysis questions about the effect of the rhyme scheme on the mood and about the details in the poem that exemplified the elements of horror. When students completed their annotations, they captured them in a photograph, and submitted the image (see Figure 4.1).

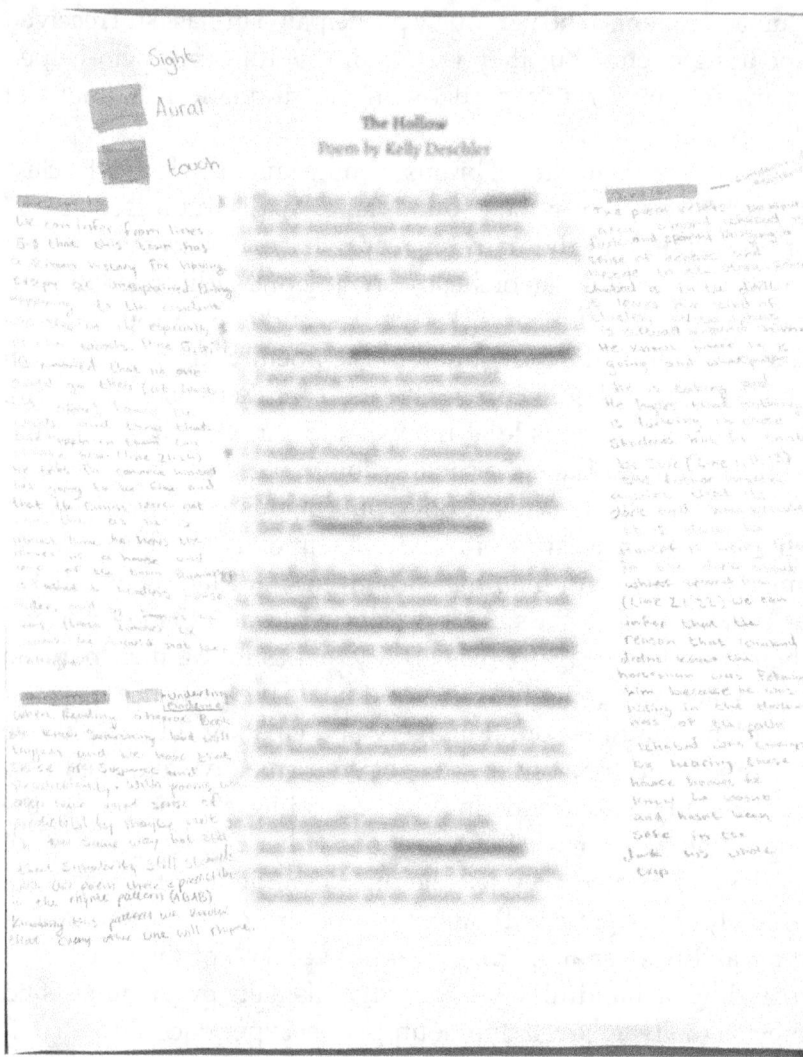

FIGURE 4.1 Student example of "The Hollow" annotations and imagery

Initially students felt bugged—even tricked—and a little put off that they had to produce a written analysis. But, as they started seeing connections between their dramatics the day before and the way their performance informed their understanding of the text, the task became an achievable challenge.

When Madison finished grading, it was clear the soundscape helped students identify the imagery—especially the aural imagery, which they highlighted the most frequently. They also drew on sound imagery to explain how the author created suspense. Multiple students noted how the main character tried "to talk himself into being okay" through his paranoia and how the sounds throughout the poem helped them better "see" what was happening. At the conclusion of the unit Madison asked students which literary device they felt the most comfortable analyzing and most chose the aural elements.

Although a few students didn't think they needed the soundscape to help them make sense of the poem, most found it helpful. In their feedback students indicated that the soundscape "made me listen more," "made me re-read," "helped me understand what was happening," and "understand the imagery in the poem." Another explained that the sounds helped her picture what it looked like to be in the hollow and "think deeper about how the sounds matched with each sentence." Yet another said she didn't know what imagery was until she connected the visual, sound, and touch elements to the soundscape. They made concrete links between the imagery analysis and the soundscape.

Soundscapes pair nicely with poetry or scenes in short stories or chapters that rely on sensory imagery to convey mood or tone. For example, the study of texts known for their intense imagery, like the short story "An Occurrence at Owl Creek Bridge" or the song of the witches from Act IV scene i of *Macbeth*, can be enhanced by the use of soundscapes. Poems like "The Raven" by Edgar Allen Poe, or "O What Is That Sound" by W.H. Auden all contain vivid auditory imagery that contributes to the mood, tone, and meaning of the poems. Many novels in verse, like *Brown Girl Dreaming*, also include passages with vivid imagery that could be highlighted with a soundscape. Other texts, such as *The Diary of Anne Frank* or Poe's short story "The Tell- Tale Heart," contain scenes where sounds play a powerful role in shaping the way the story advances. For younger students, much of Joyce Sidman's poetry—particularly those included in the collection *Dark Emperor and Other Poems of the Night*—also contain lots of poems that are enhanced by a soundscape experience.

Reader's Theater

For the next part of their inquiry into horror and mystery, Madison's students read W.W. Jacob's classic anthologized short story "The Monkey's Paw." In the short story the Sergeant-Major, recently returned from India, tells his friends about a talisman he acquired and the danger it brings because of the wishes it grants. As Madison contemplated ways to get students to engage with this text, she considered trying another soundscape. Although the tone and mood of the short story fit the horror and mystery genre, it lacked the imagery necessary to create sensory experiences in a soundscape.

But what the story didn't lack was dialogue. The plot unfolded through back-and-forth exchanges between characters. These dialogues contributed to the suspense of the story, but they also proved challenging for students to follow because they required readers to keep track of pronoun references, inferences, and subtle details. For this reason, Madison chose to use reader's theater—a strategy designed to get students into the dialogue and attending to these details.

In reader's theater, students become a part of the drama by reading the parts of different characters and sometimes even acting out the story (Black & Stave, 2007; Coombs & Young, 2014; Young & Vardell, 1993). Students each receive a script with their assignment and use facial cues, sounds, gestures, and voice inflections to convey meaning. Repeated reading helps students familiarize themselves with the words in the text, attend to details, and increase their reading comprehension (Clark et al., 2009; Keehn et al., 2009). In addition, repeated exposures build fluency, reduce anxiety in multilanguage learners (Lo, et al., 2021; Young & Rasinski, 2009), and—for students with autism—increase social awareness and understanding of other's perspectives (Keehn, 2003).

Although reader's theater often utilizes some students as actors and others as the audience, Madison wanted every student to participate and talk about the story as it unfolded. For this reason, she created a mashup that merged some aspects of reciprocal teaching with reader's theater. She began by breaking the class into groups of six to eight students. Each group functioned as its own reader's theater, with students reading the parts of the father Mr. White, the mother Mrs. White, the son Herbert White, Sergeant-Major Morris, the visitor from Maw and Meggins, and the narrator. While she separated groups of friends that tended to get off-task, she also tried to put students with peers they felt comfortable reading with and let them choose their parts.

Instead of asking students to read out of the textbook, she prepared scripts with each role highlighted in different colors. Madison embedded questions, pauses, and discussion points where she wanted the groups to stop and wrestle together with the text. For example, after the first paragraph the question required students to summarize the setting. Fifteen lines later, after three of the main characters had been introduced, students paused to list at least one attribute of each character. At one point they stopped to summarize what they knew about the talisman; at others they made predictions about what would happen when someone made a wish. The final question tied in the goals of the larger unit and asked students to consider the imagery in the conclusion and how it created a sense of horror.

As students explored these queries, they also asked their own questions and worked together to construct an understanding of the unfolding events. Here the dialogical component of the strategy became evident as students' questions not only drew them into the text to search for answers, but also facilitated an intertextual experience as they helped one another make sense of the text. One purpose of the questions included helping students understand foreshadowing. As the groups discussed the questions, they also anticipated what might come next in the story, sometimes finding just enough clues to know what to look for as they continued reading.

Although Madison admitted preparing the story into scripts and arranging students into groups required more work than asking them to read silently on their own, she felt the payoff was worth the investment. When Madison looked around the room, almost every student was "doing" the reading. In their reader's theater reciprocal teaching groups students discussed vocabulary, paused to make predictions, clarified details, and offered brief summaries that helped each other make sense of the story. Each participant followed along with their script, aware their parts might come up at any time. Instead of trying to cajole 30 students into following along with the reading, only a few needed reminders to focus. The rest engaged willingly with the text and their groups.

Students not only seemed to enjoy reading more, they also came to class energized. They focused on their parts, many read with animation and feeling, and some even read a little ahead to make sure they delivered their lines with the right emotions. For them, working in groups, reading their roles out loud, and monitoring one another as they engaged in dialogue about the text felt active and hands-on. They also felt like they had autonomy as they chose parts and participated in ways most comfortable for them. And, as each student participated in the discussion, the other students listened.

A few days later, the class settled into reciprocal teaching groups and assumed their roles as they read "The Tell-Tale Heart," stopping to discuss their own questions, clarify misunderstandings, and make predictions about what might happen in the story based on the evidence in the text. As Madison watched students working together, two thoughts occurred to her—first, perhaps she should have added "soundscape master" to their role assignments because it would have helped them more closely examine the use of sound in the text. Second, participating in soundscapes and reader's theater activities laid a foundation of reader confidence and fluency that prepared them to successfully participate in reciprocal teaching.

Short stories or chapters that demand reader attention around dialogue benefit from combining reader's theater and reciprocal teaching. "Hills Like White Elephants," by Ernest Hemingway, "Click Clack the Rattlebag," by Neil Gaiman, "A Good Man is Hard to Find" by Flannery O'Connor, "Because My Father Always Said He Was the Only Indian Who Saw Jimi Hendrix Play 'The Star-Spangled Banner' at Woodstock" by Sherman Alexie, and "7th Grade" by Gary Soto all include important dialogue that needs attention. This strategy also supports chapters or excerpts that demand a close reading to maximize comprehension. For example, it could help students better comprehend the exchanges between Aphrodite, Ares, Hephaestus, and the other gods in *Lovely War*, or a chapter from *Scythe*, where Rowan, Cintra, Scythe Currie, Scythe Goddard and other scythes meet at the Conclave and debate the future of the Scythedom.

Tableaus

After her juniors concluded reading *The Great Gatsby*, Mercedes planned to simulate a mock trial where the students tried Daisy for the murders of Myrtle Wilson and Jay Gatsby. As the prosecution and defense teams prepared opening statements and gathered evidence, Mercedes noticed that both sides relied heavily on the evidence provided in the final few chapters of the novel. However, she wanted them to pull evidence from the whole book to support more balanced, thoughtful cases. To do that, students needed a thorough review of earlier scenes. She chose a tableau activity to facilitate this review.

In tableaus students arrange themselves in different poses to create a three-dimensional depiction of an image or scene—almost like a photograph—from the text (Wilhelm, 2012). Creating this image requires students to do a close reading of the text, reading or re-reading for details to inform the way they set up the scene, including the positioning of each participant and the representation of key details. Because the strategy also requires the collective participation and engagement of the whole group, students dialogue with each other to negotiate how to represent the scene.

When the students arrived in class, Mercedes organized them into groups, and each drew a slip of paper from a basket. The papers described the type of scene the group needed to portray, but they didn't specify which scene. For instance, one paper read "Depict a scene from the novel that shows Tom is responsible for Myrtle's death" and another "Depict a scene that shows Myrtle is a victim, not the one at fault."

Before the groups staged their tableau, each needed to brainstorm 2–3 possible options of scenes within the book that met the described criteria. For example, as students considered moments in the text that would support Tom as the responsible party for Myrtle's death, the scene where Tom drives Gatsby's yellow car through the Valley of Ashes proved an obvious example. But brainstorming helped them also recall earlier moments in the novel, such as when Myrtle recounted the story of how she and Tom met. Students also remembered the scene where Wilson yelled at Myrtle and demanded to know who she was cheating with.

As the groups brainstormed and identified possible scenes for their tableaus, Mercedes consulted with each group about which scene they would ultimately portray, which also ensured minimal duplication of scenes across the class. Then students began working together to replicate the text. They consulted one another and the text itself to determine who to depict in the scene, where to position each person, and how to position them. Mercedes also asked each group to be ready to participate in thought-tracking, a strategy that pairs nicely with tableau because it invites participants to verbalize the thoughts, perspectives, and motivations of the people, objects, and elements in the scene (BYU Arts Partnership, 2022). Throughout this process, students repeatedly returned to the text to identify and negotiate their choices as they worked together to emulate the scene.

When all the groups finally completed their preparations, the tableau review began. As each group took center stage, one student wrote the description of the scene on the board. Then, with only the clues given in the description, the students in the audience worked together to summarize the scene and make connections between the group's depiction and the description on the board. Students volunteered details they remembered from the text while others offered page numbers to turn to for evidence. As the onlookers posed questions of one another, occasionally they also asked the performers questions that pertained to the scene, their behaviors, or their feelings. The participants responded to the question as the person, element, or object they depicted to help their classmates make connections between the scene and the description on the board.

As Mercedes watched the students prepare and perform, she noted that even her typically least-engaged students participated. Students expressed genuine interest in acting out the scenes and they watched as each group of their peers performed. Creating the scene and preparing for thought-tracking forced them back into the text for the purpose of the performance, but it also helped solidify their grasp of potential evidence as they took notes and prepared for the trial.

This strategy might be used at the conclusion of chapters or whole novels to summarize and review the story. It also works to facilitate close readings of particularly significant scenes within a text—for example, as students reconstruct the events at the end of Act V scene ii of *Hamlet* that led to the main character's ultimate demise or of Chapter Seven in *The Great Gatsby* where readers discover Myrtle died after being hit by a car driven by Daisy, not Gatsby. Or perhaps even when Dobby dies at the knife's point meant for Harry in *Harry Potter and the Deathly Hallows*. Tableaus also offer an alternative way for students to present their interpretations of ambiguous endings in short stories like "The Lady and the Tiger," or in novels like *A Long Way Down* or *The Giver*.

Performing Character

Performing character strategies help students use drama to consider the perspectives, motivations, and emotions characters wrestle with as they navigate the conflicts within a text (Dawson & Lee, 2018). Each of the strategies that follow invite students to slip into the role of a character and to make inferences from the text about their feelings, reactions, and motives. These performances also invite students to draw on their own life experiences as they reason through dilemmas and consider different perspectives.

Conversations with Strangers

Over 600 miles away from Mercedes, in Albuquerque, New Mexico, Marion also contemplated how dramatic strategies might help her juniors in their study of *The Great Gatsby*. After reading Chapter One, Marion taught a minilesson on common literary points of view and how point of view shapes the narrative. As practice, she gave students the opportunity to explore the limits and insights of Nick's point of view through an activity she called Conversations with Strangers (see Figure 4.2).

In this activity students sat knee-to-knee facing each other, with one person facing the front of the classroom and the other

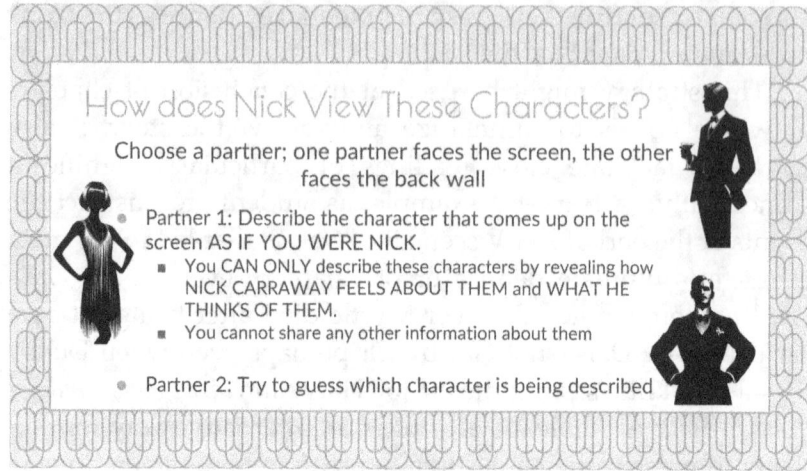

FIGURE 4.2 Conversations with Strangers discussion prompts

person facing the back of the room. At the front of the room Marion projected the image of a character on the screen. Partner One's job (the partner facing the screen) was to describe the character from the point of view of Nick, only sharing details that show how Nick feels or thinks about this person. Then Partner Two's job was to guess the character based on the description from Nick's point of view. After successfully completing a round, the two partners switch positions and Partner Two took on the task of describing the next character in the queue.

After making their way through the initial list of characters, Marion asked students to consider the following questions:

- How would you describe Nick's narration style? Is he descriptive or vague? Judgmental or generous? Biased or not? List some adjectives to describe it.
- How would this chapter be different if told through an omniscient point of view?
- What is the danger of hearing only one person's point of view of a story?

After the first day, unexperienced with the activity and with no details beyond those in the first chapter, Marion described these discussions as "initially very basic." But the class continued to practice a variation of this activity after each chapter. With each iteration of the activity, their understanding of the characters grew and their perspectives expanded.

For example, after reading Chapter Two Marion asked students to explain the apartment scene to a partner as if they were Nick, remembering to focus less on what happened and more on his feelings about the other characters—how Nick viewed their actions, the judgments he made, and the details that stood out to him in these experiences. Similarly, after reading Chapter Three students described Gatsby to a partner as if they were Nick, focusing less on information from other sources and primarily on the details Nick shared, on what Nick said and didn't say about Gatsby, and on the adjectives he used (see Figure 4.3).

The more they practiced these skills, the better students became at identifying key lines, the more adept they seemed at pulling out other evidence from the text, and the braver they became to try to participate in conversations as Nick.

After Chapter Five Marion offered a new challenge. She invited students to consider how the scene where Gatsby and Daisy meet might have been portrayed differently if Daisy or Gatsby had been narrating it. The students then selected either Gatsby or Daisy and rewrote the scene from their perspective,

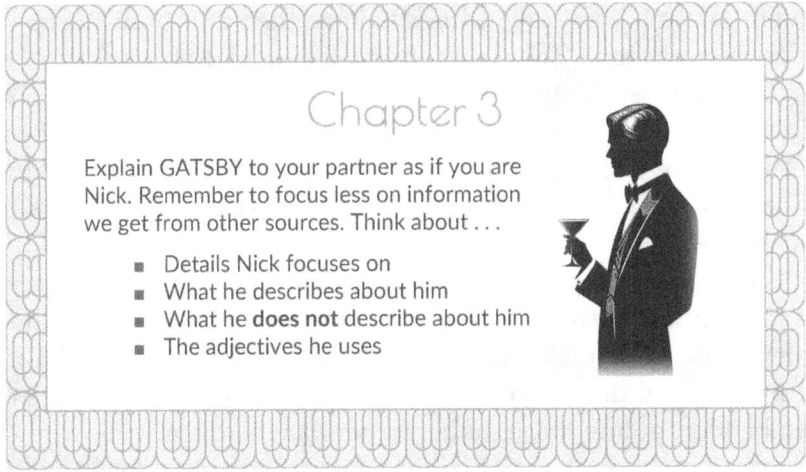

FIGURE 4.3 Conversations with Strangers Chapter 3 discussion prompt

thinking about what that character would know about their own feelings and perceptions of the meeting that others didn't, which emotions they felt, as well as which additional details they would include that Nick left out and which details would remain the same. Again, all with an emphasis on identifying evidence and using it to support their interpretations.

All this practice proved valuable for their study of point of view, but it also served as a scaffold for the perspectives and personas the students would assume in Chapter Seven when they participated in a reader's theater. In this chapter a pivotal scene occurred as Nick and Jordan witness an epically awkward exchange between Tom, Daisy, and Gatsby. Accusations fly and secrets are revealed that change the course of the narrative.

Before reading Chapter Seven, Marion put students into groups of six and students each took on one of the following roles: Nick, Tom, Daisy, Gatsby, Jordan, and Nick's narration, which filled in the gaps between the back-and-forth of the characters. After students selected their characters, Marion asked them to think about what might happen if these characters came together in the same room. "That would never happen!" one student exclaimed. "It would be a trainwreck!" another stated. "Do some predicting in your groups," she challenged. "Based on what you know about these characters, what do you predict might occur?" As students huddled together, they brainstormed possible reactions. Some thought Gatsby and Tom might come to blows. Most thought Gatsby would keep his cool while Tom flew off in a rage. Many said this would be the moment when Daisy chose Gatsby. Marion then explained that Chapter Seven revealed what happened when Daisy invited the whole group to dinner.

These activities helped prime and prepare students to engage in the action of reader's theater. On the day of the reader's theater Marion distributed the scripts, which included consolidated narration and details from the text as well as questions. Marion embedded points throughout the script where students would pause, discuss, make predictions, and pull together details from earlier chapters. With from their previous work and reading, the students assumed the personas of their characters and jumped into the text.

The students didn't disappoint. They threw themselves into the readings, using voices for different characters, and showing what they learned by projecting attributes and attitudes into their performances. Marion also noticed that as the students read, they stopped and talked about the text more. In part the questions helped, but students also authentically tried to make sense of the text, pausing to ask questions beyond those on the page and talking about the text as it unfolded. Students used evidence to support their interpretations and shared this evidence with their peers.

When the reader's theater of Chapter Seven concluded, Marion brought the class back together to debrief about the experience. Specifically, she asked students to think about their performance. Students wrote for a few minutes about a line they delivered that they felt particularly proud of, how they said it, and what they intended to convey with their tone or voice. After some discussion, Marion then invited each group to huddle together and vote on who among their group would receive the award best performance or most compelling character. Once they came to a consensus within their groups, each group presented their arguments and evidence to the whole class. These celebrations of their character interpretations provided an opportunity to recognize the great work of multiple students, revisit the passages, and attend to the the nuances that made their performances meaningful. Marion described this as an academic environment with a "sheen of fun over it."

After the class completed their reading of the novel, their final assessment involved writing a one-page response that used evidence from the text to identify who, among all the characters, proved most responsible for Myrtle's death. In preparation for this assessment, students divided into small groups and created a "Who's to Blame?" pyramid (see Figure 4.4), ranking the characters in order of responsibility.

To support their rankings, each group needed to incorporate textual evidence. Marion provided a few page numbers to help students revisit the text, but many went beyond these helps

FIGURE 4.4 The Great Gatsby "Who's to Blame?" pyramid

and also incorporated other evidence they found. Some of these quotes came from their reader's theater lines, others from their notetaking throughout the unit. Creating and defending their group pyramid prepared students to write a one-page argument with evidence explaining why they chose this particular character as most to blame.

The Conversations with Strangers strategy works well for texts where point of view plays a significant role in the storytelling. For example, short stories like "The Cask of Amontillado," by Edgar Allen Poe, William Falkner's "A Rose for Emily," "Snow," by Julia Alvarez or "The Yellow Wallpaper," by Charlotte Perkins Gillman offer students opportunities to experiment with point of view as they consider how details of the story change based on the perspective of the characters. YA novels like *Monster, Dough Boys, I Am Not Your Perfect Mexican Daughter, Firekeeper's Daughter* or *Ground Zero* also offer similarly rich opportunities. In addition, YA texts with alternating narrators like *One of Us is Lying, Loving vs. Virginia, Clap Where You Land*, or *Dreamland Burning* and middle grade novels like *Crossover, Echo, Wonder, A Long Walk to Water,* and *The View from Saturday* also offer opportunities to apply this strategy.

Variations on Performing Character: Good Angel, Bad Angel Hotseat

Hotseat strategies vary based on text and focus of the discussion, but at their core they each achieve a similar purpose: helping readers think deeply about moral reasoning, character motivations, and why people make the decisions they do. The Good Angel, Bad Angel Hotseat strategy (Garey & Blau, 2021; Wilhelm, 2012) provides a particularly effective framework for examining the motivations, strengths, and weaknesses that ultimately shape character's choices and the consequences characters face at different junctures within the text.

Mercedes began this exercise by showing her seniors a clip from *The Emperor's New Groove* (Dindal, 2000) where one of the main characters engages in a back-and-forth conversation between an angel sitting on one of his shoulders and a devil sitting on the other. After watching the clip Mercedes invited students to take out their writer's notebooks and describe a time when they felt torn between two alternatives and how they weighed the two choices. After they finished writing, a few students shared and this resulted in a whole-class discussion about the challenges people face as they consider different paths.

This writing assignment provided a segue to a discussion of Jeff Zentner's award-winning YA novel *The Serpent King*. The novel, which utilizes an alternating narrator format, tells the story of three friends at the start of their senior year—Dill, Lydia, and Travis—wrestling with weighty decisions that will shape their individual and collective futures. Throughout their study of the first third of the novel, students paid particular attention to these decisions, marking the huge choices facing the three main characters.

As they entered class earlier that day, each student pulled a slip of paper out of a basket that read "Dill," "Lydia," or "Travis." After completing the writing exercise and discussion, they self-sorted into groups based on the name written on their paper.

Within these groups, the students reviewed the decisions facing their assigned character throughout the first third of the novel. Should Dill stay in Forrestville and work at the grocery store to pay off his father's debt or leave town and go to college? Should Lydia leave Forrestville, cut ties with her friends, and not look back as she starts a new life in NYC, or go to college and split her life between her old and new friends? And Travis—should he try something new like football? Enter the military after high school? Continue to work at the lumber yard?

Students then broke into smaller subgroups to consider the implications of each choice, why the character might be drawn to these alternatives, and how the character might rationalize each option (see Figure 4.5).

As the groups worked through the wrestles of their character, Mercedes noticed that every student—even those typically reluctant to participate—got involved and spoke for their side. After the subgroups developed their rationales, students lined up on either side of their classmate representing the character. The student playing the part of the character chose which angel to listen to first, inviting them to share the "right" choice from their perspective and to explain why. Sometimes the character engaged the angel in discussion, but each only had 45 seconds of talk time before they switched, and the character engaged with another perspective. When the angels on both sides ran out of reasons, the character explained which side seemed most convincing and why.

Some of the rationales students shared focused on issues facing both themselves and the characters in the novel. For instance, many students emphasized the importance of listening to trustworthy people invested in their success. Miguel, a student had who already enlisted in the military and planned to head to boot camp a month after graduation, talked about the importance of doing things outside his comfort zone and keeping a part of himself while exploring other life options. Simon—another student in the class—related to Travis's dilemmas in the novel, expressing that he too felt happy living a quiet life and questioned if everyone needed to do big things after high school.

Angel vs. Devil on Your Shoulder

For this assignment, you will be choosing one person in your group to act as Dill. Then, the remaining group members will divide up between the "angel" and the "devil." Talking to the class member acting as Dill, you will try to convince him to choose your side. You will be demonstrating the two sides, and the thinking, to the class when the preparation timer runs out. Whoever is the character will be choosing a side at the end of your presentation.

Your character: Dill

Conflict: Post-High School Decisions
- #1: Stay and work to help your parents pay off their $270,000 in debt. You will be working in the grocery store you currently work at now.
- #2: Leave Forestville and go to a college somewhere.

Angel vs. Devil on Your Shoulder

For this assignment, you will be choosing one person in your group to act as Lydia. Then, the remaining group members will divide up between the "angel" and the "devil." Talking to the class member acting as Lydia, you will try to convince him to choose your side. You will be demonstrating the two sides, and the thinking, to the class when the preparation timer runs out. Whoever is the character will be choosing a side at the end of your presentation.

Your character: Lydia

Conflict: Post-High School Decisions
- #1: Leave Forestville and everything there behind. You have a lot of new friends already, and you won't have to worry about friends making you feel guilty for living life.
- #2: Leave Forestville and try to keep relationships with those back in Forestville; have a split life between your new world at NYU and your life in Forestville.

Angel vs. Devil on Your Shoulder

For this assignment, you will be choosing one person in your group to act as Travis. Then, the remaining group members will divide up between the "angel" and the "devil." Talking to the class member acting as Travis, you will try to convince him to choose your side. You will be demonstrating the two sides, and the thinking, to the class when the preparation timer runs out. Whoever is the character will be choosing a side at the end of your presentation.

Your character: Travis

Conflict: Senior Year Decisions
- #1: Do what his dad wants him to: try something new by playing football and possibly entering the military at the end of high school
- #2: Continue to read his fantasy books, chat on his forums, hang out with his friends and do what he feels comfortable and happy doing

---

FIGURE 4.5 Good Angel, Bad Angel Hotseat instructions

Students based their contributions on the evidence in the book, but they also incorporated their own beliefs and background experiences into their reasoning. Their own perspectives, beliefs, fears, and concerns could not *not* impact the direction of the discussion and the decisions being made for the main characters. For example, one of the students representing Lydia concluded by stating Lydia should cut off her friends and move forward. Then she added, "This is also actually my answer for my own life because I'm going out of state for college and it's almost more stressful for me to think about keeping relationships with people here." This also happened as other students crafted rationales explaining what their characters should do. Students repeatedly saw their personal dilemmas reflected in the dilemmas of the characters and put themselves in the characters' positions as they considered how to move forward.

In these ways, Mercedes observed the Good Angel, Bad Angel Hotseat strategy made the book more relevant to her students, particularly as they found themselves wrestling with similar choices about life after high school. As students shared their rationales for the perspectives they represented, they not only drew on ideas from the book to support their options, but also incorporated rationales generated using evidence from their own lives. Across two classes of seniors, students presented distinctly different rationales and no two main characters selected the same options at the end of the discussions. The variety of responses across classes evidenced the way diverse students drawing on their unique backgrounds and interpretations of the text resulted in a variety of understandings, discussions, and experiences with the story.

In other texts, weighing options is less about good and bad or right and wrong, and more about the alternatives characters face as they find themselves at hinge points. Consider Ethan and Maddie in *Ethan Frome* as they wrestle with the decision to sled or not to sled into the tree. Should George shoot Lennie in *Of Mice and Men*? What is the best way for Connor, Risa, or Lev to resist their individual and collective fates in *Unwind*? What about Odilia and her little sisters on their Odyssey-like adventures in *Summer of the Mariposas*? Or Amil and Nisha in *Amil and the After* as they navigate starting life in a new country?

Variations on Performing Character: Conscience Alley

Like Good Angel, Bad Angel Hotseat, Conscience Alley gives students the opportunity to consider the different options and alternatives available to a character in response to a dilemma or conflict (Dawson & Lee, 2018). As with the previous strategy, students select a person to represent the character at the crux of a vital decision. The rest of the class considers the character's options and decides which choice they will advocate for, making an argument for their perspectives or drawing quotes from the text to advocate for their positions.

In the debrief and reflection component of this approach, the teacher invites the student who walked down the alley to share how they felt listening to the different rationales and perspectives, as well as what made some of the voices more persuasive than others. The rest of the class might also share which voices caused them to reconsider their points and why. During this recap consider also asking students how this process compares with their own decision-making processes when they find themselves at a crossroads.

Variations on Performing Character: Character Lines and Tone

In preparation for a reader's theater or the Conversation with Strangers strategy, this activity can be used to help students explore character attributes and prepare students to engage in character analysis. Begin by distributing a list of emotions to each student as well as a few sentences. Put students in pairs and ask them to take turns reading their sentence with different emotions on the list. For example, consider how the sentence, "I can't believe that he took her to the dance last night!" might be read with anger, sadness, joy, or frustration. Encourage students to practice a variety of emotions with different tones and emphases.

Next, give each pair a description of a character from the novel or play. These descriptions should include not just physical attributes, but also personality traits that help students understand the character's values, feelings, motivations, and behaviors. Ask them to study the description and identify emotions on the list or chart they would associate with that character. Then, invite them to practice reading that same sentence after the manner of their character. An extension and additional scaffolding would include then giving students lines or quotes from the character that will appear in the text and asking them to try reading these lines the way their character would say them.

The debriefing discussion can explore inferences students made about the characters, predictions about the character, potential conflicts, or their interactions with other characters. In addition to helping frontload information about characters, this strategy also helps ease students into participating in other dramatic strategies, particularly those students more reticent to engage. For example, before reading plays like *12 Angry Men, A Raisin in the Sun, The Glass Menagerie,* or *A Midsummer Night's Dream,* this strategy helps familiarize students with the characters and prepare them to read with emotion. Or, for novels where character development is a key component of the instruction, such as *The Outsiders, The Book Thief, Speak, Long Way Down* or *Genesis Begins Again,* this activity can help students with character analysis and assist them in keeping track of the variety of characters within the novel.

Considerations

Dramatic strategies offer students opportunities to use action, sounds, and movement to interpret texts and construct meaning. As students work together, drawing on their background knowledge, experiences, and interpretations to enact or represent meaning, they engage with the text in deep, substantive ways. Perhaps most significantly, these strategies help students better understand the perspectives of others in ways that expand their own worlds. Maryanne Wolf (2018) explained that,

> Perspective taking not only connects our sense of empathy with what we have just read but also expands our internalized knowledge of the world…Through this consciousness-changing dimension of the act of reading, we learn to feel what it means to be despairing and hopeless or ecstatic and consumed with unspoken feelings.
> (p. 45)

The power and importance of feeling and consciousness changing is harnessed through dramatic strategies. Soundscapes help students understand imagery and experience the mood and tone of a text. Reader's theater brings students into the story as they use their voices and gestures to bring narratives to life and support their comprehension. Tableau representations force students to revisit texts, attend to details, and discuss the implications of details in a scene or plot. Performing character strategies help students attend to the details and nuances of characters as these strategies place students in the shoes of the characters.

Although dramatic strategies offer tremendous benefits, they don't require significant time investment on the part of the teacher. This is, in part, because they place the responsibility for "doing" the reading on the students. Tableaus, soundscapes, and most performing character strategies require the students to return to the text, to find the details, and to negotiate what those details mean for the products the students will create. Several fantastic teacher resources highlight other dramatic strategies worth integrating into the curriculum (see Text Box 4.1).

Perhaps the greatest challenge with dramatic strategies centers on helping students understand what it means to represent or embody characters in ways that don't perpetuate stereotypes and respect diverse cultures. For example, what might it mean for two white students to read dialogue written in African American English spoken by two black characters in culturally respectful

---

TEXT BOX 4.1   Additional resources for using dramatic strategies

Edmiston (2014). *Transforming teaching and learning with active and dramatic approaches: Engaging students across the curriculum*. Routledge.

Dawson and Lee (2018). *Drama-based pedagogy: Activating learning across the curriculum*. Intellect.

Garey and Blau (2021). *Theater, drama, and reading: Transforming the rehearsal process into a reading process*. NCTE.

Wilhelm (2012). *Deepening comprehension with action strategies: Role plays, text-structure tableaux, talking statues, and other enactment techniques that engage students with text*. Scholastic.

ways? What kind of cultural awareness should teachers create to help students understand the nuances of culture, race, and socioeconomics as they engage in Conversations with Strangers from the perspectives of Mrs. Price and Rachel in Sandra Cisneros' short story "Eleven?" What boundaries and behaviors are appropriate when representing characters on the margins in dialogue and enactment? In addition to the texts themselves, these and other similar questions should be the focus of dialogue among teachers and students considering these strategies.

Finally, as Madison demonstrated, these strategies can be used together to help scaffold and orchestrate meaningful engagement with the texts. Using soundscapes and reader's theater seemed an obvious and natural fit with short texts in a unit examining mood, theme, and tone. Consider how character lines and tones would prepare students to participate in a reader's theater of *The Importance of Being Earnest*, followed by a reader's theater of Act I and then a conscious alley activity to examine the choices available to Algernon, Gwendolen, and Jack. Or even Conversations with Strangers to introduce the characters in *Furia*, followed by a Good Angel, Bad Angel Hotseat for Camilla at different points in the narrative as she contemplates the myriads of choices facing her.

These examples offer just a few possibilities for combining strategies to help teach concepts and engage students in meaningful dialogues about the perspectives and issues represented within texts. But what might this look like even beyond the use of dramatic strategies? What other combinations and scaffolds provide opportunities to engage students with reading and dialogue about texts? The power and possibilities of using multiple dialogic strategies to engage students and facilitate deep reading experiences not only with drama, but with artifacts, simulations, and other experiential opportunities is the focus of the next chapter.

References

Black, A. & Stave, A. (2007). *A comprehensive guide to readers theatre: Enhancing fluency and comprehension in middle school and beyond*. International Reading Association.

BYU Arts Partnership. (2022). *Drama [Website]*. https://advancingartsleadership.com/node/10#21redhotprocessdramatools

Clark, R., Morrison, T. G. & Wilcox, B. (2009). Readers' theater: A process of developing fourth-graders' reading fluency. *Reading Psychology, 30*(4), 359–385.

Coombs, D. & Young, T. (2014). Blending informational texts and readers theatre to promote authentic inquiry. *English in Texas, 44*(1), 9–14.

Dawson, K. & Lee, B. (2018). *Drama-based pedagogy: Activating learning across the curriculum*. Intellect.

DeBlase, G. (2005). Teaching literature and language through guided discovery and informal classroom drama. *English Journal, 95*(1), 29–32.

Dindal, M. (Director). (2000). *The emperor's new groove [Film]*. Walt Disney Pictures.

Douglass J. & Guthrie, J. (2008). Meaning is motivating: Classroom goal structures. In J. Guthrie (Ed.) *Engaging adolescents in reading* (pp. 17–32). Corwin.

Edmiston, B. (2014). *Transforming teaching and learning with active and dramatic approaches*. Routledge.

Garey, J. & Blau, S. (2021). *Theater, drama, and reading: Transforming the rehearsal process into a reading process*. NCTE.

Juzwik, M., Borsheim-Black, C. Caughlan, S., & Heintz, A. (2013). *Inspiring dialogue: Talking to learn in the English classroom*. Teachers College Press.

Keehn, S. (2003). The effect of instruction and practice through readers theatre on young readers' oral reading fluency. *Reading Research and Instruction, 42*(4), 40–61.

Keehn, S., Harmon, J. & Shoho, A. (2009). A study of readers theater in eighth grade: Issues of fluency, comprehension, and vocabulary. *Reading & Writing Quarterly, 24*(4), 335–362.

Lo, C., Lu, S., & Cheng, D. (2021). The influence of reader's theater on high school students' English reading comprehension-English learning anxiety and learning styles perspective. *SAGE Open, 11*(4), 1–7.

Rosenblatt, L. (1978). *The reader, the text, the poem: The transactional theory of the literary work*. Southern Illinois University Press.

Wilhelm, J. (1997/2008) *"You gotta BE the book": Teaching engaged and reflective reading with adolescents*. Teachers College Press.

Wilhelm, J. (2012). *Deepening comprehension with action strategies: Role plays, text-structure tableaux, talking statues, and other enactment techniques that engage students with text*. Scholastic.

Wolf, M. (2018). *Reader, come home: The reading brain in a digital world*. Harper.

Young, C. & Rasinski, T. (2009). Implementing readers theatre as an approach to classroom fluency instruction. *The Reading Teacher*, *63*(1), 4–13.

Young, T., & Vardell, S. (1993). Weaving readers theatre and nonfiction into the curriculum. *The Reading Teacher*, *46*(5), 396–406.

5

Integrating Dialogical Approaches

While JC's middle schoolers studied the people, places, and events depicted in the graphic novel adaptation of Steve Sheinkin's nonfiction text *Bomb: The Race to Build—and Steal—the World's Most Dangerous Weapon*, JC experienced his own epiphany about dialogical strategies. One day at the beginning of their inquiry, JC read the text aloud to the students, inflecting feeling into his voice as he read the speech bubbles scattered among the images and text boxes. At this point in the story, Oppenheimer and other scientists began their descent upon Santa Fe, New Mexico, noticeably shocked by the primitive working conditions in this remote town. As scientists began streaming into the office of an overworked secretary, phones rang off the hook and soundbites of unintelligible conversations filled the speech bubbles in each panel.

JC began reading the part of the secretary as she said, "Come in! Yes. I'm holding…" simultaneously talking on the phone and nodding a welcome to yet another scientist walking in the door. But when JC approached an image of a phone ringing off the hook, he hesitated slightly. Should he read all of those "riiings!" coming out of the phone?

Then, from the back of the room, Maurice shouted out, "You gotta do the noise Mr. Leishman!" JC hesitated. Before he could respond, Maurice began. "Riiing!" Then Joey chimed in. "Riiing!"

JC continued to read as Maurice and a handful of other students made the phones "ring" in the background. At that moment a sudden insight occurred to JC. "This is a soundscape!" he realized. The simultaneous ringing amidst the dialogue more accurately conveyed the chaos in the panels than any single reader could portray. The students were hooked on the collaborative reading approach…and so was JC.

Eventually JC and the class set up a system, a mashup of sorts that combined reader's theater and soundscapes. One or two students read the captions that described the setting of the story or that introduced the characters and details of the narrative. Other students read the thought and dialogue balloons for the characters, helping tell the story through internal and external dialogue. The remainder of the class created sound effects throughout the story—from phones ringing to bombs exploding and everything in between.

As they read together, integrating components of soundscapes and reader's theater supported comprehension of, and engagement with, the story. Creating the soundscape generated renewed excitement in the text for some students and situational interest in the act of reading for others. Fulfilling their reader's theater roles helped students focus on their lines, especially those responsible for creating sounds. In hindsight, pairing soundscapes and reader's theater seemed an obvious and natural fit for graphic narratives because the text features lent themselves to the almost effortless distribution of parts and whole class participation in the reading.

But opportunities to combine dialogic strategies go beyond those used by JC and the other combinations alluded to in Chapter 4. In addition to the intertextual experiences described in previous chapters, a range of stimulating tasks provide an almost endless combination of dialogical learning approaches to engage students in dynamic reading experiences. This chapter explores possibilities for integrating dialogical strategies across units to create content-rich instruction and classroom talk anchored in significant texts and inquiries.

Why Integrate Dialogical Approaches to Teaching Reading and Literature?

The examples and illustrations shared throughout this book demonstrate how intertextual experiences that utilize stimulating tasks trigger emotions, questions, and interest in students. These responses help students develop situational interest in content-rich texts as students seek answers to questions as well as connection with characters, conflicts, and themes. This kind of learning inspires students to engage dialogically with texts, one another, and the world.

The strategies and approaches highlighted in previous chapters demonstrated the use of stimulating tasks to motivate otherwise disinterested students to read. These tasks proved valuable not only for the immediate situated interest they generated, but also because repeated and frequent integration of these tasks fosters lasting, intrinsic motivation. As the researchers explained, "When students experience multiple situational interests in reading, accompanied by perceived competence, autonomy, or relatedness in reading activities, then students increase their intrinsic reading motivation" (Guthrie et al., 2006, p. 244). In other words, students' motivation increased as they participated in opportunities to make reading hands-on, autonomous, relevant, and social.

Interestingly, the applied nature of dialogical approaches to teaching reading and literature makes them inherently hands-on, autonomous, relevant, and social. Intertextual experiences value hands-on explorations and media to support the construction of meaning. These intertextual experiences also include insights and connections recounted by teachers and classmates that build context to help readers comprehend texts. Each of these "texts" supports student learning by introducing new ideas, situating new concepts within familiar contexts, and valuing students' cultures and background knowledge. Building this familiarity fosters a sense of relatedness to texts and topics (Guthrie, 2008). These connections to students' own lives and interests then increase motivation.

The discussion and argumentation intrinsic in dialogical strategies also motivates students to engage in meaningful discussions with their peers about content-rich topics. As students actively listen to one another, receive and respect multiple perspectives, and allow one another time to process, they participate in dialogic speaking and listening practices (Juzwik et al., 2013). This co-construction of knowledge builds relatedness within the classroom, both with other students and with the teacher. In addition, students building and relying on relationships with others fosters comprehension (Applebee et al., 2003). These social connections support student learning and help increase reading growth.

Finally, content-rich instruction that values student autonomy offers choice and opportunities for students to share their learning. When students transform texts into genres and representations of meaning that relate to their experiences, it "allows for a deeper understanding, and possibly more important, a deeper enjoyment" (Douglass & Guthrie, 2008, p. 25). Whether formal or informal, these approaches to assessments connect students' feelings and experiences with texts. In addition, allowing students to identify personal meaning in the text and assessment leads to an increased sense of competence.

Generating feelings of autonomy, social connection, and relevance also proves key because, as Travis pointed out in Chapter 1, students' feelings about words and ideas are integral to their reading engagement. As neurophysiologist and educator Carla Hannaford (1995) explained,

> Our mind/body system learns through experiencing life in context, in relationship to everything else, and it is our emotions, our feelings that mediate that context. In order to learn, think or create, learners must have an emotional commitment. Otherwise, education becomes just an intellectual exercise.
>
> (p. 56)

Stated differently, emotions and feelings are essential to students' investment in learning. Integrating multiple dialogical strategies across a unit helps generate feelings of autonomy, relevance, and sociality that sustain student interest throughout the unit and sometimes beyond.

Applications and Examples of Dialogical Strategies in Tandem

JC's epiphany that introduced the chapter demonstrated one way to utilize multiple dialogical strategies to engage students in the study of literature. The countless possible combinations of texts, strategies, students, and curricular expectations make it impossible to offer surefire formulas for creating such moments. But examples of these strategies working together can inspire teachers with ideas to adapt to their own classrooms. The examples in this chapter illustrate ideas for integrating dialogical strategies throughout units. In addition, text boxes and commentary included throughout invite you, the reader, to think metacognitively about the way intertextual experiences anchored in content and paired with dialogue support student learning and provide autonomy, relevance, and sociality.

Transforming Text to Meaning with *Bomb*
As soon as the classroom set of *Bomb: The Race to Build—and Steal—the World's Most Dangerous Weapon* arrived, students immediately asked JC "Are we reading this?" The book itself proved motivational for the students already consuming a steady diet of graphic novels. For them, the opportunity to study one in class seemed too good to be true. For other students, those who had never even looked at a comic, the possibility seemed slightly more daunting. But JC knew that in either case, students needed to explore the repercussions of the atomic bomb and a develop a deep understanding of the text itself to wrestle with the question "Was it ethical for the US to drop the bomb?"

Intertextual Approach Utilizing a Stimulating Task: Time Machine Experience
In order for students to engage in ethical reasoning, JC needed to contextualize the people, places, and events that drove the narrative. When students arrived in class on the first day of the unit, JC explained they needed to travel back in time to the 1950s and experience a few facets of life critical to understanding the conflict at the heart of the novel. They loaded into their "time machine" (which looked very similar to their classroom),

JC pushed some buttons, and they ultimately found themselves in the 1950s, taking notes on artifacts they examined as well as experiencing a few common practices.

Their 1950s experience began with a viewing of the cinematographic masterpiece *Duck and Cover*, produced by the US Department of Defense (Middleton et al., 1952). This film featured Bert the Turtle modeling the proper response in a nuclear explosion for school-aged children—primarily to duck and cover (see Figure 5.1).

The students took notes and then, at the film's conclusion, JC asked them to summarize their observations. Essentially everyone came to the same conclusion—to avoid the peril of a nuclear attack, duck and cover. To drive the point home, JC introduced the second 1950s experience: a nuclear siren. Like the students in the film, JC's students practiced how to "duck and cover." JC played the nuclear siren and, when they heard the signal, everyone got under their desks and wrapped their arms around their heads and necks.

After a successful practice or two, JC showed the class the third piece of 1950s history: actual footage of a nuclear bomb

FIGURE 5.1 Image from the film *Duck and Cover*, produced by the US Department of Defense

detonating—including the flash of light, paint vaporizing from surfaces, buildings incinerated, trees blowing sideways, and other ripple effects of the destruction. After watching the footage, JC invited the class to consider the effectiveness of the duck and cover strategy. He asked, "In reality, do you think 'duck and cover' would do much?" The class discussed why getting under their desks might help avoid the effects of the shockwave, but also the futility of this behavior at ground zero. Some students hypothesized that the government made the video to instill a false sense of security in citizens, while others questioned some of the recommendations in the context of 2024.

> *In the Time Machine experience, JC employed visuals, enactments, and sounds to provide intertextual experiences that helped students contextualize the impact of the bomb in the lives of people at this time. These activities created relevance. Then, the discussion and critical analysis that followed helped students connect the experiences to the novel and to critique the ethics of using these weapons.*

Intertextual Approach Utilizing a Stimulating Task: Spy Hunters

Their time machine experience complicated students' understanding of the event at the heart of their inquiry, but students also needed to understand some of the complexities of World War II and the major players around the globe who were involved. This knowledge proved particularly necessary in terms of the characters in the novel. To introduce the players and help students develop a strong understanding of their characteristics, JC utilized a simulation he called Spy Hunters.

JC organized students into groups of four or five and gave each a dossier of information about one of the major characters in the graphic novel. It included a photograph of the character, a headshot from the graphic novel, a description of the character, and a list of reasons they may or may not be a spy. For example, the dossier on Albert Einstein included both real-life and illustrated images, a paragraph describing him as a German Jew who worked as a physicist and immigrated to the US. Possible reasons he might be a spy included his German heritage, his lifelong commitment to pacifism, and his preference for socialism. In contrast, he was likely not a spy because of his Jewish heritage, the letter he wrote to President Roosevelt recommending the construction of the atom bomb, and his US citizenship.

Students received their dossiers and talked through the evidence, summarizing their findings and interrogating the validity of the arguments for or against each character's potential guilt. When they arrived at a consensus, they rated the character's spy potential on a scale of one to five. Then the group received a new dossier and repeated the procedure. Once they reviewed and ranked all the files, each group explained who they identified as the likely spy.

This activity did not ruin the ending of the novel for the students because Sheinkin identifies Harry Gold as the real spy in Chapter One of the graphic novel. Instead, it helped acquaint students with the characters and their roles in the central conflict. This activity frontloaded information that helped students better follow the developing plot and make inferences as they encountered each character in the text.

> *JC also saw the Spy Hunter Simulation as an opportunity for students to learn how to work in groups, a foundational skill essential in successful reciprocal teaching activities and literature circles, two dialogical strategies JC would use later in the unit. Sociality provides motivation, but it also requires students to take responsibility for their learning. This activity gave students a chance to demonstrate their ability to stay focused, be accountable, use evidence to make arguments, and talk with one another until they arrived at a conclusion. If (or when) students struggled in one of these areas, JC offered individual interventions or whole class mini-lessons to support this and future group-focused experiences.*

Content-Rich Reading and Writing: Soundscapes, Reciprocal Teaching and Discussion

As exemplified in the introduction, throughout the unit some of the reading occurred together as a class, utilizing a soundscape and reader's theater combination to work through the text. On other days, JC organized students into small groups and used reciprocal teaching to work through the text. In addition to their reciprocal teaching roles, some groups chose to add the reader's theater component, where one person read the captions, a few read the dialogue, and the remaining members read the sound effects. Whether reading as a whole class or in small groups, at the conclusion of each chapter students summarized what they read.

> *Read, Talk, Write is another dialogical strategy that could be used when reading in small groups or pairs. Here's how it works: Before beginning, mark the text into sections, possibly by subheadings or paragraph chunks. Then, pair students up and identify a Partner A and Partner B in each pair. At the teacher's signal, Partner A begins reading aloud as Partner B listens. When partner A finishes reading, Partner B summarizes what happened in the section Partner A read. When Partner B finishes summarizing, both write one or two sentences summarizing what they just read. Then the partners switch jobs and Partner B reads the next section out loud and Partner A summarizes. When students finish reading the entire text, they have short summaries of each section that identify the most important points in the text.*

Intertextual Approach Utilizing a Stimulating Task: Legacy of the Bomb

JC also included a series of assignments called "The Legacy of the Bomb" interspersed throughout the reading to help students understand the ramifications of the development and detonation of the atomic bomb. At different points in the reading these intertextual experiences supplemented the whole-class and group readings of the novel. The first included a YouTube video called *The Most Radioactive Places on Earth*, featuring footage of radioactive locations around the world and Geiger counter measures of their radioactivity levels. The images and information in this video helped students better understand the long term environmental and human impacts of nuclear explosions.

The second intertextual experience occurred midway through the book, right after the Trinity test. After the countdown concluded and readers turn the page, a giant mushroom cloud filled the panels. At this point JC pulled up a computer simulation called "Nukemap" that allowed users to drop a pin anywhere in the world, then simulate detonating a nuclear weapon in this location (Wellerstein, 2018). Depending on the size and strength of the weapon, a map then showed the approximate radius of the radiation, fireball, heavy blast damage, light blast damage, and thermal radiation from the bomb as well as estimated casualties. JC shared this simulation after the bomb drop in the book to show students the impact of the bomb at the Trinity test site and then to simulate what would happen if the bomb was dropped on the small Idaho where they lived. As students looked at the two maps and the devastation sank in, the bell rang and class concluded.

A third inquiry included a visual prop box. Small groups of students received a series of images—pictures of the Hulk, Godzilla, the videogame *Fallout*, and novels from two YA series, *The Hunger Games* and *Michael Vey*. As students reviewed each image, they tried to identify its relation to nuclear energy. For instance, nuclear scientist Bruce Banner became the Hulk after exposure to gamma radiation. Different versions of the Godzilla story identify nuclear explosions as the source of the monster's power and even of Godzilla himself. But other connections went deeper than just pop culture, such as parallels between the way Katniss Everdeen and Michael Vey distrusted the government and how Robert Oppenheimer's conversation about disarmament with President Truman led him to similar conclusions.

> *The video, image prop box, and bomb blast simulation each provided an intertextual experience for students that prompted discussion about events or issues central to their understanding of the text. In contrast to the intertextual experiences described earlier, these activities did not take large amounts of planning. However, they did offer moments of connection with the text that built relevance and situated learning within the contexts of students' own lives and interests.*

Intertextual Approach: Using Evidence to Support Multiple Perspectives and Creating an Epilogue

For their final assessment JC's students created their own graphic novel-style epilogue for *Bomb* that answered the question "Was it right to drop the bomb?" Throughout the unit JC intentionally integrated still and animated images of the people, settings, and events in the story to help students see the value of images to convey meaning. Now it was their turn to apply this learning to their own work.

JC broke the assessment into parts, first asking students to answer the question "Do you think it was necessary for the US to build the bomb?" and to give three reasons in support of their answer. Students could draw on their chapter summaries and evidence from the book. As they considered their perspectives, students discussed their reasons and rationales with one another. These dialogues included the sharing of evidence, points, counterpoints, and ideas. These discussions led some students to revise their position and other students to find stronger evidence in support of their perspectives.

> *To help students brainstorm possible answers for this assessment, activities like Good Angel, Bad Angel hot seat or Conscience Alley could help them consider a variety of stances they might take, as well as viewpoints that might be represented in the epilogue. These strategies offer both autonomy and opportunities for students to learn in dialogue with their peers as they form their own opinions and beliefs.*

Next, students considered how to represent these perspectives in their own graphic epilogues. Their final products needed to include twelve or more panels with at least five informational boxes, three lines of dialogue, and one sound effect. Their epilogues needed to not only summarize parts of the chapters, they also needed to be grounded in the actual story and refer to actual characters or events in the story. For example, Anya wrote from the perspective of Lona Cohen. Hector wrote his from the viewpoint of the Japanese Emperor.

Others told theirs from the perspectives of a survivor of the Hiroshima bomb, as a pilot who dropped the bomb, and even as two classmates in 2024 discussing the morality of dropping the bomb (see Figure 5.2).

Jessica Douglass and John Guthrie (2008) explained that to produce sufficient dialogue with texts and develop comprehension, students needed to reflect and create personal connections to characters through journaling or other representations in mediums that allowed them to look through the eyes of the characters. The duck and cover experience and Nukemap simulation made the threat of an atomic bomb personal. The dossiers acquainted students with characters and also taught them to question the motives of each character. The soundscape and reader's theater immersed readers in the text itself as they participated in engaged reading. And the graphic epilogues students wrote and illustrated allowed them to represent perspectives and positions that reflected their own beliefs about the explosion. Throughout this unit the intertextual experiences, discussions, and, ultimately, the final project provided students with opportunities to personalize the text as they considered their own answers to the inquiry.

Whole-Class Integration of Approaches: Must...Have...Chocolate
Almost any teacher will tell you that inspiring learning between the end of November and mid-January is tough. After seven years of teaching 6th grade English language arts (ELA), Jeanie knew that her noble attempts often proved no match for the magic (and sugar) of the holiday season. However, she also knew tapping into the festivities offered a powerful motivation to drive student learning—*if* she could craft an inquiry unit that capitalized on some aspect of students' lives and interests.

But what might that inquiry be? Over the last 15 years, the once-rural and relatively homogeneous farming population of Enumclaw, Washington welcomed an influx of immigrants from India, Ukraine, and various countries in Latin America. The increasingly diverse neighborhoods, community traditions, and flavor preferences around town offered opportunities to open students' worlds to the lives and cultures of the people around

FIGURE 5.2 Graphic novel-style epilogue final assessment

(Continued)

FIGURE 5.2 (Continued)

them. Jeanie wanted to celebrate the diverse traditions, customs, and cultures of all her students and then she realized the topic that brought together the season, the traditions, and the community: food.

Intertextual Approach Utilizing a Stimulating Task: Prop Box

When students walked into class the Monday after Thanksgiving break, they curiously eyed the eight foods displayed: onions, apples, Theo's chocolate, Tim's Cascade Chips, Aplets & Cotlets, salmon, Starbucks coffee, and Almond Roca (see Figure 5.3). Although no one seemed eager to bite into the onion, before class even started students' conversations and questions revolved around the foods.

The bell rang and Jeanie launched their inquiry by asking students to identify the common link between these foods in a think–pair–share. As she walked around the room listening to their conversations, their guesses ranged the gamut: "Maybe we are sorting them–healthy or unhealthy?" guessed Kayla. "They all have some kind of wrapping." observed Lorenzo. "She's going to cut the onion in front of us to make us cry," accused Liam.

FIGURE 5.3 Washington food items prop box

The class continued brainstorming, but it wasn't until Jeanie projected a caricature map of Washington State that a few students shouted, "These are Washington foods!" Students then took turns explaining each food's relation to their state. Ashlyn described getting a drink from the world's first Starbucks in downtown Seattle. Kody and Juaquin talked about seeing the salmon run on fishing trips. Tyrell recounted the flying fish at Pike Place Market, which led to lots of questions and a YouTube detour to show other students the famous fish throwers.

> *The intertextual experience came not just from the food prop box that initiated questioning and an introduction to the unit. It also came as Jeanie invited students to share their stories about the foods. As they recounted their understandings of each food's relation to their state, they built a collective text that all students could draw on to support their comprehension. The sharing of stories also built relatedness and relevance, as demonstrated in the next section.*

Intertextual Approach: Inviting Stories

Next Jeanie asked students to define the term "folklore." Some ventured guesses while others looked up definitions that all coalesced around ideas of customs, traditions, and cultural elements of a group. The class then considered a definition for "folk foods" and hypothesized: Food passed down through generations? Food significant to a region because of its availability?

Jeanie then invited them to reflect on their food experiences over the break and food traditions they looked forward to during special holidays. She asked, "What foods absolutely, positively had to be on the table to make this time special?" Students huddled and shared in groups before transitioning to sharing with the whole class, which opened the floodgates to stories. Instead of prying responses out of students, typically quiet kids shared of their own volition. Others who lacked confidence in their academic abilities and often remained silent during discussions chimed in—in large part because almost everyone had family food traditions to share.

The discussion soon shifted to other ways culture and food transacted. Jeanie moved students in and out of groups in a conver-stations rotations to continue the dialogue. In conver-stations (Wessling, 2024) groups of four to six students are presented with a question and respond by sharing evidence and experiences. After five minutes, one or two students from each group rotate to different groups and each new group begins discussing a new question related to the first. In this case, questions like "When are times food plays a significant role in culture?," "How does our culture wrap itself around food?," and "What other roles does food play in our culture?" After five minutes, two more students from each group rotate and the process begins again.

> *The conver-stations strategy provided a way for many students to contribute to the collective understanding of concepts like "folklore" and "folk food." This strategy also built relatedness as they discussed topics they could each be an expert in because they drew on their personal experiences. Notice that in almost every instance, Jeanie's intertextual approaches are followed by discussion or argumentation that reinforces the content-rich instruction.*

In response to these questions, some groups talked about dinner as time for families to connect. Similarly, others talked about the value of friends sharing lunch. Many groups identified food as essential to celebrations. Others described food as expressions of love at times of death, birth, and sickness. Still others took a critical approach, discussing food scarcity and food waste that sometimes occurs in these moments. Students also interrogated questions about the cost and time of food preparation, and even food in hunter and gatherer times compared to the modern era.

Intertextual Approach: Video and Argumentation that Values Using Evidence to Support Multiple Perspectives and Interpretations

After re-capping the major takeaways from their food culture discussion, they watched a video highlighting a variety of school lunches from across the globe. In just under six minutes, meals from over 20 countries flashed across the screen. Afterwards, students shared their opinions, critiquing the representation of US school lunch and questioning others. The Indian students talked about the Indian lunch and shared observations about the extent to which their families ate traditionally Indian versus Americanized meals. The Latinx and Ukrainian students shared similar insights. As students filed out of class, Jeanie heard many continuing the conversation and bemoaning the state of their own lunch that day.

Content-Rich Vocabulary Instruction: Word Specialist Tea Party

Their next session included a vocabulary tea party to introduce terms in the reading. The tea party strategy typically involves teachers or students choosing words, quotes, or questions from a text, writing them on a notecard, and then mingling with classmates to crowdsource answers to questions or to discuss quotes (Beers, 2002). In this cause, Jeanie's students each received a word highlighted on a list of other terms from the reading. Each student became a word specialist as they looked up definitions, synonyms or antonyms, examples of the word in context, or other clues to help them explain the word and the concept it represented (see Figure 5.4).

After determining the meaning of their assigned words, students began mingling, their lists and clipboards in hand. They searched out other students who researched words on the list they didn't know, such as cacao, inedible, conquistador, indelible, plantation, conundrum, decedent, and Aztec. When they found a specialist who knew the meaning of an unknown word, students taught one another and recorded their discoveries.

Once students felt confident in their knowledge of the words, they returned to their seats and examined their notes.

Below are words that you may not be very familiar with from a chapter we will be reading over the next two days. Your job is to learn the highlighted word on your list and record clues to help you teach it to others. Then take your clipboard and walk around, looking for people who can teach you the words you need. You only get ONE definition from each person. When you have ALL the words, please sit down.

word	What this word means	parts of this word I recognize	images of this word	some synonyms of this word are	some antonyms of this word are
delectable					
inedible					
Equator					
Aztec					
conquistador					
invigorating					
decadent					
plantations					
conundrum					

Now that you know what all the words mean, what do you think this chapter is going to be about? Explain why you think that.

FIGURE 5.4 Vocabulary tea party list

The final assignment that day asked them to consider their word collections and then use those words to make a prediction about the chapter. Students combined the different concepts into a myriad of possibilities. Armed with these understandings and predictions, they felt prepared to launch into the reading the next day.

> *As each student studied their words, their sense of competence increased. Students also saw one another as resources to support their learning, which fostered a sense of relatedness and competence. In what ways did the video viewing and discussion of the "Lunches Around the World" video offer a similar type of experience for students?*

Content-Rich Reading Instruction: There Is No Ham in Hamburgers

The following day, the smell of chocolate wafted down the 6th-grade hallway, sparking students' curiosity and drawing them toward Jeanie's classroom. As they walked through the door, the smell lingered in the air and their eyes locked on trays of chocolate filled cupcake liners covering the counters. They fired questions at Jeanie, but she let the anticipation build. She knew anything out of the ordinary created suspense that added to the overall effect of her strategy.

Jeanie began class with a brief book talk on *There's No Ham in Hamburgers*. This nonfiction text by Kim Zachman featured ten tasty chapters exploring the histories of, and mysteries behind, some of the most popular foods in the US. Each chapter included text boxes with supplemental information, illustrations, "chew on this" facts, recipes or experiments for hands-on learning, and selected sources for curious researchers to explore.

As they previewed the text, Jeanie explained they would start by reading a chapter together and engaging in some activities. Students scanned the chapter titles and students blurted out their preferences, but the smell of chocolate and Jeanie's schoolwide reputation as a chocoholic made it clear which chapter their teacher had chosen.

Together they opened to "Chapter Nine: Must...Have...Chocolate" and students followed along as Jeanie read. The chapter began by describing the Aztec discovery of cacao when the god Quetzalcoatl descended from heaven and taught the people how to transform cacao beans into a thick drink. Jeanie paused and used a map to show the Aztecs' region, inviting students to share their knowledge of the Aztecs. Then they read a text box about cacao trees and discussed the difference between cocoa and cacao—specifically the contrast between the raw ingredient and the chocolate eaten today.

> *Each chapter in this book offers an engaging nonfiction reading experience that prompts inquiry into popular foods relevant to preteen culture. In Jeanie's unit this text grounded the inquiry, but the inquiry question also invited students to participate and contribute in ways that honored their home cultures. In these ways, the inquiry provided built in relevance and opportunities to foster relatedness and competence.*

Intertextual Approach Utilizing a Stimulating Task: Taste Test

Jeanie then proposed an experiment to help them understand the difference between cacao and cocoa. She grabbed a tray from the counter filled with cupcake liners containing cacao nibs. Expressions of skepticism, excitement, and uncertainty punctured the room as students waited for Jeanie to distribute nibs. Some students eyed the nibs warily, while others noted that they looked like chocolate shavings. A few smelled the nibs and commented on their resemblance to dark chocolate. Others felt the texture and noticed the nibs didn't melt. Once everyone had a sample, Jeanie counted down, "Three...two...one...bottoms up!" They collectively experienced the taste of pure cacao as some students threw back the contents of their cupcake liners, while others cautiously sampled a few nibs at a time.

Expecting something sweet, some students shuddered at the bitterness of the taste. Some said they loved it. Others took satisfaction in their peers' reaction when they showed no reaction. But everyone had something to say about the cacao. "Why did the Aztecs like this?" "Why would they drink it?" "Why doesn't this taste like chocolate?" Their reactions turned into a barrage of questions and their questions led them back to the book, both for answers and because they wondered what experience might come next.

> *Touching, smelling, and tasting the cacao nibs offers a unique variation of artifactual experiences because of the heightened sensory experience it offered. In addition, as the class encountered the nibs together, they participated in a shared experience that built relatedness among the students and with the content.*

The chapter then described a beverage called "cacahuatl" or "cacao water," a strong, bitter drink seasoned with chili pepper revered by the Aztecs. Then when the Spanish Conquistadors conquered the Aztecs, they took the drink back to Spain and replaced the chili pepper with sugar. They called it "chocolatl," or "cocoa water." Several students who struggled in ELA but loved history shared their knowledge of the Spaniards and answered questions raised by their classmates. This provided extra comprehension support for the rest of the class and gave the students doing the sharing a chance to shine.

As the class engaged in this discussion, Jeanie distributed the next round of samples. Only then did the students realize the rich aroma wafting down the hallways came from her crock pot full of warm, chocolaty liquid. Their experience with the cacao nibs caused some students slight trepidation about this substance, but as Jeanie proclaimed, "Bottoms up!" the class drank. Comments like "That's delicious!" were met with questions like "That tastes normal to you?" and exclamations of "I'll finish yours if you don't want it!" Some connected the drink to the text, identifying the flavor as hot cocoa seasoned with chilis. Many students with Latinx heritage said "Hey, we drink this at the holidays!," noting its similarity to traditional drinks shared by their families and giving some multilingual students a sense of authority as well as a chance to contribute their expertise to the discussion.

> *Similar to tasting the cacao nibs, drinking the chocolatl and the discussion afterward fostered relatedness. It also gave the students familiar with the drink an opportunity to demonstrate authority and competence concerning the subject at hand.*

Intertextual Approach Utilizing a Stimulating Task: Chemistry Experiment

The following day, after the previous round of reactions and questions subsided, the class returned to the text. The next section took a scientific turn, highlighting the century-old culinary challenge that faced cacao consumers who tried to mix cacao paste with water. The class read about the experiments of Dutch and French chemists who tried to transform cacao from a drink to a consumable bar. When the text explained it took these men another 28 years to successfully invent milk chocolate, Jeanie asked if anyone knew the cause of this conundrum. The scientifically savvy students ventured a few guesses and Jeanie directed them to a text box that explained why chemistry prevents the oil in chocolate from mixing with the water in milk. She then distributed jars filled with oil and water that provided a visual of the separation in real time.

Intertextual Approach Utilizing a Stimulating Task: Polling and Math Applied

The next section described the origins of two iconic American chocolate brands: Hershey's (creator of Hershey's Kisses) and Mars (originator of candy covered M&Ms). To preface this section, Jeanie created a Google form survey with three questions: 1). What is your favorite candy bar? 2). What is the most popular candy bar in the class and what percentage of students do you think prefer this bar? and 3). What is the most popular candy bar in the 6th grade? As an incentive, Jeanie promised the student who most accurately guessed the answer to question two would win a candy bar of their choice.

To determine the winner, the 6th grade math teacher joined the fun and turned the data into a math problem. She walked students through the steps to calculate percentages and explained how math applied to this real-life situation. Not only did this integrate content from another discipline into the lesson, but the data collection allowed each student to share personal preferences that pertained to the reading. Students didn't need to be strong readers or knowledgeable about the content to participate in the survey or be eligible for the prize, but the contest and the mathematical connection heightened interests for many.

> It's easy to think of experiments like these as the work of math and science classes, but they can also provide engaging intertextual experiences in ELA as well. What other types of experiments might offer hands-on learning opportunities to support comprehension?

Intertextual Approach Utilizing a Stimulating Task: Battle of the Bars

After the students calculated the results to the survey, they read the section about how the Hershey's and Mars candy companies came into existence. The conclusion of this section included a few paragraphs exploring competition within the candy bar market, which led them to their final experience: a face-off between Hershey's and Mars called the "Battle of the Bars." In this last taste test of the day, each student received two squares of chocolate—one in a green cupcake holder and the other in a pink holder. Before beginning, Jeanie instructed students on the procedures. She told them to place the first chocolate on their tongue and let it melt into their senses. Once it melted, they swirled it around in their mouths, experiencing the texture and taste of the chocolate. She then urged them to take a huge whiff through their nose to connect the smell to their sensory experience.

Some students laughed or giggled, which only encouraged Jeanie's over-the-top performance. But most sank into the experience, testing the first chocolate, then the second. At the conclusion of the taste test students completed another Google form and voted for the chocolate either in the pink or in the green cupcake holder. After the results came in, Jeanie revealed the identities of the chocolates, with Dove (a Mars product) emerging as the overwhelming favorite. The class period ended with conversations about their chocolate discoveries.

Content-Rich Reading Instruction and Discussion

After modeling deep, engaged reading in the chocolate chapter, Jeanie invited students to become specialists on the other chapters and teach the class what they learned. Students divided into self-selected groups, and each chose one of the remaining chapters until every one in the book was covered. Then students huddled together and took turns reading sections out loud. As they read, they took notes and discussed concepts to include in their presentations.

On the last day of classes before winter break, the time for presentations arrived. Jeanie used the chocolate chapter to create some slides and model general expectations for the presentations. Each included a hook, a summary of the key ideas, and whole-group participation. Although not a requirement, many of the groups brought foods and artifacts to supplement the information they shared. For example, the group that presented "Chapter Seven: Peanut Butter Better" made peanut butter blossom cookies. Another group presented "Chapter Five: A Hot Dog by Any Other Name" and shared samples of homemade deer sausage. For these students, adding food to the experience made the ideas in the text come alive.

> *While Jeanie's students didn't use a formal reading and discussion protocol to facilitate talk about the text, either reciprocal teaching or Read, Talk, Write would have provided a structured framework for focusing their small-group reading experiences and discussions. Or, instead of sharing their learning through class presentations, students could participate in a jigsaw with members of other groups. These practices provide scaffolded supports that help students understand how to participate with one another.*

Intertextual Approach Utilizing a Stimulating Task: Sharing Food and Family Histories

On a particularly icy January morning after winter break, Jeanie arrived at school with bags of flour, eggs, milk, and sugar. She lugged them into the faculty lunchroom, and was joined a few minutes later by a parent volunteer. The two got to work mixing and baking. A half an hour later, as students started filing in, the parent kept cooking and Jeanie walked across the hallway to start first period.

Then Jeanie announced the culminating assignment for their study of food traditions and folklore: students would write about their own food traditions. She began by sharing a model, her own food narrative for the class about Swedish pancakes (or "pans," as her family called them). Her narrative began by detailing the story of her Uncle Ben making Swedish pans at the annual family reunion and the origins of this tradition, which dated back to her great-grandparents who immigrated to Washington from Sweden. The next section explained the history of the thin pancakes in Sweden, including text boxes that offered supplementary information.

Then the class paused their reading and walked across the hall to sample Swedish pans covered with butter, powdered sugar, and syrup, courtesy of the parent volunteer. They drizzled, dipped, and enjoyed their own taste of Swedish pans, then came back to the classroom and reviewed the rest of the text, which included a family interview, images, and a recipe card.

> *When Jeanie shared her stories in the classroom, she modeled the expectations for the assignment and created a space for students to share their stories. This not only helped build community, it also helped students see how they could write about things they knew and loved in a demonstration of their literacy skills.*

The students then used the chapters from the book and their teacher's example to create a list of "must have" and "could have" characteristics for their own food narratives (Dean, 2021).

For instance, based on the models, students knew they needed a personal statement that described their relationship with their food, including an explanation of how the food came to hold an important place in the student's family and a history of the food's origins beyond their family. By examining the structure of the food narratives, they recognized important characteristics that made the narratives distinct and informational, including section headings, facts or trivia boxes about the food, and recipes. These requirements were added to the assignment sheet (see Figure 5.5) and for the next week students researched and wrote their narratives.

On presentation day, the classroom filled with energy and a cacophony of smells as students prepared to share their work. Each took turns presenting their recipe cards and describing the importance of their food traditions in their families or communities. The class listened with rapt attention—in part because of Jeanie's watchful eye, but also because students truly engaged with one another's presentations.

Kateryna, a Ukrainian refugee, wrote about dumplings called "pelmeni," all in Ukrainian. Andrea described a cake made of chocolate wafers, whipped cream, and pulverized candy canes integral to three generations of her family's Christmas traditions. The title of Advik's chapter "Rice Pudding Used to Never Have Rice!" sounded like one from the book itself and described the kheer his family ate at Diwali. Hector explained the history of tamales his family enjoyed at major celebrations. Ella made her feelings about her family food tradition clear in her title "Disgusting Christmas Ribbon Jell-o," a seven-flavor Jell-O tediously layered one on top of the other. Skyler brought in spätzle, a homemade noodle with cheese his family ate generations ago in Germany. Josh, whose parents came from indigenous tribes in Alaska, brought in "pilot bread"—a staple in many villages when bread isn't readily available (see Figure 5.6).

From the introductory day through the final celebrations, Jeanie integrated a variety of dialogical strategies to stimulate students' interests and connect the content to their own lives. As students participated in intertextual experiences such as taste tests, experiments, polls, and collaborative inquiries, Jeanie used

FIGURE 5.5 Food narrative assignment sheet

think–pair–shares, small-group work, and other discussion strategies to get students talking. These experiences capitalized on the active, social elements of the class while also allowing students to participate in their own learning. Throughout the unit Jeanie modeled the kinds of reading and writing she expected students to do. Ultimately, the final projects exemplified students' ability to apply research, writing, and presenting skills while celebrating their cultures, heritages, and lives.

> *Jeanie knew that research said creating space for students' home cultures in the classroom would support her ML students and students who traditionally struggled. Including students' cultures and interests in this unit provided a space for these students to share what they loved and fostered relatedness among all of the students.*

Candy Cane Cake from the VanValey Kitchen

9 oz Nabisco Famous chocolate wafers (Dewey's Bakery: Brownie Crisp cookies)

16 oz heavy whip cream

50-100 mini candy canes, crushed

Unpackage candy canes and place in gallon freezer bag. (Double bagging is beneficial to avoid peppermint dust from getting on work surface) and hammer until candy canes are very small. Beat whipped cream in a glass bowl until stiff peaks form. (Freezing the glass bowl for an hour prior helps the whipping process.) Fold in candy cane bits and dust. Spread a tsp of whipped cream onto each wafer. Stack wafers together creating a log, standing on edge on a serving platter. Frost with remaining whipped cream and refrigerate at least 4 hours. Cut dessert diagonally and serve.

KHEER

4 CUPS OF FULL CREAM MILK
5 TABLESPOONS OF ORGANIC SUGAR
½ TEASPOONS OF CARDAMOM
¼ CUP RICE
ALMONDS AS MUCH AS DESIRED
CASHEWS AS MUCH AS DESIRED
2 TABLESPOON SWEET RAISINS
¼ TEASPOON SAFFRON

WASH THE RICE, THEN GREASE A HEAVY/DUTCH OVEN AFTER THAT POUR MILK AND BOIL IT ON A MEDIUM FLAME. AFTER THE MILK IS HOT OR BOILING, ADD THE RICE AND STIR IT. KEEP IT ON LOW HEAT UNTIL THE RICE IS SOFT OR A LITTLE MUSHY. DURING THIS, BE SURE TO BE STIRRING. WHEN YOU ARE DONE ADD YOUR 5 TABLESPOONS OF SUGAR (YOU CAN ALWAYS ADD MORE OR LESS TO SUIT YOUR TASTE). LOWER THE FLAME AND COOK TILL THE SUGAR DISSOLVES COMPLETELY AND THE RICE KHEER TURNS THICKEN. AT THIS STAGE YOU CAN TASTE TEST AND ADD MORE SUGAR IF WANTED. NEXT ADD THE CARDAMOM, SAFFRON AND STIR. WHEN SERVING ADD ALMONDS, CASHEWS, SWEET RAISINS
ENJOY YOUR DESERT!!!

FIGURE 5.6 Student samples of recipe cards from their food narratives *(Continued)*

Aloo ke Sabse — How to Make

Ingredients:
- 2 tablespoons oil
- 1 teaspoon of carom seeds
- ½ cup of chopped onions
- 2 teaspoons, finely chopped ginger
- 1 teaspoons of finely chopped garlic
- 1 or 2 green chillies
- 1 cup chopped tomatoes
- 2 cups diced potatoes
- ½ teaspoon turmeric powder
- 1 spoon red chilli powder
- ½ Garam Masala
- 1 pinch of asafoetida
- 1 teaspoon of dry mango powder
- 2 cups of water
- 2 tablespoons coriander leaves- to garnish

Heat oil in a 2 litre stovetop pressure cooker. Add the carom seeds and fry them for a couple of seconds. Now add the chopped onions and sauté them till soften on medium-low heat.

Add the ginger, garlic and green chilies and saute for a few seconds till the raw aroma of the ginger and garlic goes away.

Add the chopped tomatoes and saute till the tomatoes become soft and pulpy.

Add the turmeric powder, asafoetida and red chili powder. Mix well.

Now add the diced potatoes. Add salt and mix well.

Add water and pressure cook the curry on medium heat for 3 to 4 whistles or till the potatoes are done.

When the pressure drops naturally in the cooker, then only open the lid.

Open the lid and simmer the curry by pressing a few cooked potatoes with the spoon on the sides of the cooker.

This is to get a slightly thicker consistency of the gravy. The starch from the aloo make the gravy a little thick.

Once done, sprinkle some garam masala powder and mango powder. Mix well and garnish with some coriander leaves.

Poori for 15-18 poori's

Ingredients:
- 2.5 to 3 cups whole wheat flour
- 1 tablespoon of oil
- water - to knead the bread, add as required
- oil- for deep frying, as required

Knead the wheat flour into a stiff dough with water and oil. Make small balls of the dough. Roll into rounds having 4 to 5 inches diameter.

Heat oil for deep frying. Fry the pooris in medium hot oil till they get puffed and are golden brown. Remove them into paper napkins to remove excess oil. Fry puri in batches.

FIGURE 5.6 (Continued)

Integrating Approaches Using Stations, Centers, and Differentiated Assessment

"So, when do we start the project?" Ricky asked as he walked into his 12th grade English class. His teacher Kaylee looked surprised, then smiled. "I thought you didn't like the book?" she playfully retorted, remembering his reluctance after reading the first chapter. "Well…" Ricky's words trailed off. "Chapter Two was not that bad. And I've been thinking about some ideas for my project," he explained.

Earlier in the year, when Kaylee outlined the curriculum for her semester-long mythology class, she hoped reading and exploring classic myths would engage her diverse class of over 30 seniors and stave off their symptoms of senioritis. White, Black, Latinx, Indigenous, cisgender, transgender, IEPs and exceptional—collectively, the class claimed a diversity of labels and identities. Although their individual commitments to academics ranged considerably, at this point most did not consider school as their top priority. For this reason, in addition to high-interest texts, Kaylee tried to integrate a variety of strategies that required student investment. Her class frequently participated in gallery walks, jigsaws, artifactual inquiries, reciprocal teaching, and other approaches where students actively played a part in their own learning.

For their final unit of the semester the class recently began exploring the question "What challenges do we encounter and how do we overcome them?" as they read Gary Schmidt's YA novel *The Labors of Hercules Beal*. If this title sounds familiar, it's because in Chapter 1 of this book I described the perils the main character, Hercules Beal, faced as he worked to complete a year-long assignment from his ex-Marine-turned-English-teacher, Lieutenant Colonel Hupfer. Like Kaylee's seniors, the fictional 7th graders in Lieutenant Colonel Hupfer's class were studying mythology. And, both Kaylee and Lieutenant Colonel Hupfer sought to include dialogical approaches to learning in their curriculum that required students to explore and experience the implications of ancient myths in their own lives.

Intertextual Approach Utilizing a Stimulating Task: Stations that Promote Dialogue

To launch their exploration and introduce key elements in the novel, Kaylee prepared stations (Harvey et al., 2019; Pho et al., 2021). In stations, small groups of four to six students rotated through different activities designed to introduce or supplement the unit inquiry. Set up in various spaces around the room, each supported students' understanding of, or engagement with, an element of the text. Kaylee wanted to make the stations as dialogical as possible, so she intentionally designed them around intertextual experiences that introduced the text. Students spent 15–20 minutes working with their classmates to accomplish tasks at their assigned station and then recorded their findings on the graphic organizer before rotating to the next station and beginning their next tasks.

Quote and Comment. At the first station students took turns reading quotes from the novel, then discussing their responses to the quote. For example, one quote read, "It's easy to love what loves you back…I guess it's a lot harder to love what doesn't love you back" (Schmidt, 2023, p. 240). After the discussion, each recorded their thoughts about the quote and how it pertained to their lives on their graphic organizer. Then they moved on to the next quote and repeated the routine.

Character Predictions. This station featured five groups of images and artifacts to introduce the characters Hercules, Achilles, Viola, and Lieutenant Colonel Hupfer, and key plot points in the novel. Students looked at each set of items and made predictions, then recorded their predictions on their graphic organizers.

For instance, Lieutenant Colonel Hupfer's slide contained a silhouette of a military figure, a stack of books, a chalkboard, and Greek columns (see Figure 5.7).

Students ventured guesses such as "Is this a military school?" or "Are we reading a war story?" Then they reviewed the next slide and repeated the process. When they saw the image of a dog on the Hercules slide, they wondered, "Is this a book where something happens to the dog?" These images primed students with knowledge and predictions they could consider and revise as they encountered each character in the novel.

Personal Journaling. At this station students explored one of the central themes of the book by reading a quote from the novel from Hercules Beal about how fast life can change for the bad, but also its potential to change for good. It read, in part:

> …everything can change in one millimillionth of a second…I guess we live knowing that things can change,

FIGURE 5.7 *The Labors of Hercules Beal* character prereading station

but acting like they're not going to. I'm not going to act like that anymore. I know things can change in a millimillionth of a second. That means bad stuff sometimes. But maybe it can be good stuff too. Maybe I can help it mean good stuff sometimes.

(Schmidt, 2023, p. 142)

After they read and pondered, students wrote individual responses to the question "What have been some of the 'labors' in your life so far? How have they taught or changed you (for good or for bad)?" on their graphic organizers.

> *These stations represent just a few of the many intertextual experiences Kaylee could have used to introduce the novel. For instance, consider a station that featured prop boxes and quotes for each character or a station that asked students to create tableaus of different scenes. In addition to whole class stimulating tasks, a number of artifactual and dramatic strategies work as stations. And, the small group feature of stations provides built in opportunities for discussion, argumentation, and sociality. Kaylee also noted that the sociality provided peer pressure for students to put their phones away and engage with the task.*

These types of prereading activities work well in stations because they access students' background knowledge and help connect their experiences with the reading without requiring direct instruction from the teacher.

Content-Rich Reading and Writing: Brainstorming Project Proposals

For the first two chapters the class listened to the audio and followed along in their books. As they read, they revised their predictions from the day before, noticing details about each character. But after the first chapter some students expressed skepticism about the novel, stating that Hercules reminded them of annoying younger siblings, or that the text didn't deal with the kinds of challenges they faced.

However, in Chapter 2 as Lieutenant Colonel Hupfer gave his speech about the Classical Mythology Application Project, their interest shifted. Then Kaylee revealed they—like the students in Lieutenant Colonel Hupfer's class—would be completing their own Classical Mythology Application Projects. In their version, students would research a myth of their choice, identify the main themes, and develop a mythology application project related to their myth. For example, in the myth of "Hades and Persephone," themes might include "mother and daughter relations, parental control, and toxic relationships." For their project a student might research healthy relationships and share their findings in a series of social media posts or volunteer at a women's shelter. At that point, the seniors were hooked.

As students brainstormed, their ideas ranged the spectrum. Kaden, a student whose parents recently divorced, chose the story of Perseus, which explored loyalty and betrayal in relationships. He wanted to interview his grandparents about how to maintain healthy, long-lasting relationships. Themes of love conquers all and the potential of enemies to become lovers exemplified in the myth of Cupid and Psyche resonated with Valerie, a teen who recently transitioned and experienced less-than-kind reactions from family and friends. She chose to show intentional love and kindness to everyone she encountered for a single day.

Next, they completed project proposals that included a few key parts. First, the name of the myth and main characters; second, a description of the project, including what the student would do, how other people would be involved, and where the project would take place; third, a timeline; and finally, a discussion of anticipated concerns and questions for Kaylee. By the end of the day, each student had selected a myth, identified its themes, and proposed at least one potential project idea.

> In Lieutenant Colonel Hupfer's assignment, he chose the myth and identified the project for each of his 7th grade students. Kaylee gave her seniors the autonomy to choose a myth meaningful to them and to propose their own projects. In both cases the teachers anticipated the projects would simulate a learning experience for the students that embodied the themes of the myth, but in a less dangerous real-life situation. Therefore, in each case the teachers also vetted the projects for learning potential and feasibility. Consider the recommendations in Chapter 3 for simulations. How might those apply to these projects as well?

Intertextual Approach Utilizing a Stimulating Task: Research Centers

Although Kaylee's students had spent all semester reading and exploring different myths, they needed structured support as they embarked on their analysis and projects. Kaylee wanted students to engage with the stories and to talk with one another about their findings, but the individualized nature of the projects necessitated that students work at different paces and sometimes with different focuses. For this reason, she used research centers to structure their writing and honor student autonomy.

Centers allow students to independently practice skills or accomplish tasks that don't need direct instruction and to help students take responsibility for their own learning (Frankel, 1975; Movitz & Holmes, 2007). Unlike stations, where students work through each space in structured rotations, in centers students move from space to space independently, choosing where to spend their time to complete the required tasks.

In this case, she designed the centers to help students analyze their myths. Students moved about with Chromebooks in hand, using their planning sheet to guide where and how they spent their time. At one center they identified their myth's characters, creatures and symbols. At another they described the setting and wrote a detailed summary of the story. Another center required them to reflect on changes that happened to the character, make inferences about the myth's themes and tropes, and connections to modern society. And finally, at another center they identified additional sources to explore.

> *The centers Kaylee designed here helped focus students on their independent research. But centers can also be used for artifactual inquiries and to explore different ideas. The key to both centers and stations is the focus. If students need direct, explicit instruction to succeed at the station or center, then the activity will be more successful in whole class or small group instruction. If the activity is reinforcing learning that has already taken place or inviting students to draw from and dialogue about their own experiences, stations or centers can be viable options.*

As students worked at their individual centers and recorded their answers, Kaylee conferenced with them to make sure they each had a plan to move forward with their projects. At the conclusion of class each student completed an exit ticket answering this question: Based on your reading and research, how does this myth connect to our society at large and your life individually?

Intertextual Approach Utilizing Stimulating Tasks: Gallery Walks, Jigsaws and Stations to Support Content-Rich Reading Instruction, Dialogue, and Reflection

After Chapter 2, each of the remaining chapters in the novel focused on the original labors of Hercules and Hercules Beal's adaptation of it. For this reason, Kaylee utilized dialogical strategies that helped students understand the original labors alluded to in the chapters as well as the lessons both Herculeses learned.

Gallery Walks. Chapters 3 through 6 featured the first four labors of Hercules: slaying the Nemean lion, killing the nine-headed Lernaeaon Hydra, capturing the Ceryneian hind, and catching the boar of Erymanthus. Before beginning their reading, students participated in a gallery walk where each of the four classroom walls featured "exhibits" about these labors (Daniels, 2011). Students read and reviewed the information, artifacts, images, and videos displayed, then synthesized their learning into summaries of the labor and the strengths Hercules gained, recording their responses on their graphic organizers (see Figure 5.8).

Then, over the next few days, the class read the four corresponding chapters, both as a whole class and in reciprocal teaching groups. Students spent time talking with one another about similarities between the labors performed by Hercules and Hercules Beal, identifying examples of how these growth experiences resonated with their own lives.

Jigsaw Groups. for Chapters 7 through 10, Kaylee organized jigsaw groups. In jigsaw groups, students participate in a home group and an expert group (Aronson, 2002). Kaylee's students began by meeting in their home groups to review the four labors that needed to be studied. Then they each moved to their expert group to read and summarize one of the next four labors: cleaning the Augean stables, slaying the Stymphalian birds, capturing the Cretan Bull, or stealing the Mares of Diomedes. Then back in their home groups they shared their summaries of the labor with each other. Finally, over the next few days, students read each of the chapters, each assuming responsibility for one of the reciprocal teaching roles and stopping to discuss the text and record their responses.

Stations. Kaylee created stations containing intertextual strategies for the final four-chapter sections—one station for each remaining labor—that helped students make predictions or generate connections to the Herculean labor and Hercules Beal's experience. For example, at the station where they learned about Hercules obtaining the belt of Hippolyta, students used

In the graphic organizer below, keep track of what's happening with the 12 labors!
- You will fill out the first two boxes <u>when we go over the original myths as a class.</u>
- You will fill out the bottom two boxes <u>when we read that assigned chapter!</u>

<u>What was the original labor?</u>	What were the main lessons learned or strengths gained?
How did Hercules Beal adapt this labor? What lessons/strengths did HE gain?	What are some ways this labor (or its lessons and potential for growth) have shown up in your life? List 3-6 examples

FIGURE 5.8 *The Labors of Hercules Beal* graphic organizer

reciprocal teaching to read the myth and discuss their questions, predictions, and understandings. At the station for the labor of stealing three golden apples of Hesperides, the group completed a mini jigsaw with a description of the labor divided into six parts. They each chose one of the six parts and became the "expert" that could explain their part to the group.

The next station features a Jackdaws collection for the labor of obtaining the cattle of the giant Geryon. They made predictions about this labor, recorded them on sticky notes, and then compared their predictions with the text as they read. At the stations for the final labor—bringing Cerebus back from Hades—students role played a scenario similar to the situation Hercules Beal faced in Chapter 14. Based on the scenario and their knowledge of Hercules, they predicted how he would react, then read the labor, and compared it with their initial predictions.

> *Kaylee described the use of jigsaws, prop boxes, dramatic strategies, and reciprocal teaching in stations as "inception" because it involves the use of strategies within strategies that all come together under the umbrella of the unit's mythology application project. This setup was also only possible because her students had participated in each of these intertextual experiences as a full class. They knew what to do from previous experience, so they could work autonomously at each station.*

Substantive Reflections. After every fourth chapter, students wrote longer, in-depth reflections, like those Hercules Beal wrote after each labor. In these reflections they returned to their graphic organizers, identified an insight or parallel between one of the four most recent labors of Hercules Beal and their own lives, and then expounded on this connection in 150 or more words (see Figure 5.9).

Kaylee managed these reflections similar to the way Colonel Hupfer did and, like the students in the novel, Kaylee's students complained about the word count. However, they enjoyed identifying similarities between Hercules Beal's experiences and their

Reflection #1

Circle which labor you're reflecting on:

Lion   Hydra   Hind   Boar

In 150+ words, write your own narrative reflection on an experience or an insight you've had that parallels the labor you've chosen, similar to what Hercules did!

_____

_____

_____

_____

_____

_____

_____

_____

_____

_____

_____

_____

_____

FIGURE 5.9 *The Labors of Hercules Beal* reflection sheet

own lives and these shorter reflections helped them practice the kind of reflection required in their final projects.

Intertextual Approach Utilizing a Stimulating Task: Mythology Application Projects

After students completed their initial project proposal, they continued to read in class and work on their projects outside of class. Throughout the unit Kaylee utilized exit ticket check-ins and student conferencing to ask questions such as "What do you need help with?" and "Where are you in the process?" Students reported their progress and executed plans for engaged meaningful applications of their myths' themes.

Like any project, some students took greater advantage of the opportunity than others, but many students used their project to process and reframe challenges in their own lives. Sonia found links between Medusa's story and themes of hope amidst lost identity, abuse, and consequences. Angelo, a soon-to-be first-generation college student, studied the Norse myth of Ragnarök, a myth of a massive, universe-altering event that everyone prepared for. He saw applying to and attending college as a similarly significant event in his life that he needed to prepare for, so he crowdsourced information about the application process from his peers, school counselors, and others. Jaden, still struggling with his father after his parents' divorce, chose the story of Daedalus and Icarus. This myth's themes of pride and the negative traits a father passed on to his son inspired Jaden to create a series of video messages to his future children about generational cycles he promises to break.

> *A few of the stimulating tasks that drove the unit took place in the traditional school day, but the stimulating task at the heart of the inquiry occurred outside of school and was student-led. These types of stimulating tasks also offer opportunities to foster relatedness between students and the text as well as autonomy as they tailor the tasks to their own interests and passions.*

Artifacts, Stories, and Multiple Perspectives: Dialoguing and Reflecting on Learning

When the day came for students to share their projects, each student brought an artifact that represented their project and a written summary describing their project's connection to the myth and their lives. The artifacts included video clips, audio recordings, photographs, and other tangible representations of the projects.

Kaylee organized students into small groups of four, allotting 10–12 minutes for each to share their artifact and a summary of their project, including the easiest and most challenging parts of the experience. Most of the students seemed comfortable sharing their work and receptive to that of their classmates, sharing across social groups, interest groups, and other differences.

However, as Kaylee scanned the room, she wondered if perhaps she was asking too much of some of them. For example, she eyed a group that contained two popular boys and two quiet and reserved girls. What had she been thinking when she put that group together? But as the choir girl shared her recording and lyrics, the boys offered genuinely supportive affirmations. This seemed to be the case in each of the other groups as well, with students asking meaningful questions and listening intently to their classmates.

After the sharing, students completed a reflection on their classmate's projects as well as on their own Classical Mythology Application Projects. They noted things they appreciated about each project and then wrote a final reflection (like the one Hercules wrote at the conclusion of his labors) bridging the gaps between the novel, their myths, and their lives.

> Both Kaylee and Lieutenant Colonel Hupfer knew that reflection provided the key to helping students see connections between their studies and their own lives. The reflections Kaylee embedded throughout the reading of the text helped prepare students to complete the longer, substantive reflection on their projects. This kind of scaffolded instruction prepared students for success and helped them be more metacognitive about their learning.

As Kaylee read the responses from her very diverse group of students, she realized that although the focus of their experiences and projects varied greatly, completing these projects helped break down barriers among students and create bridges of understanding in the class. Whatever the focus of their project, each demanded vulnerability and connection with their peers. After the sharing of projects, their final whole-class discussion revisited the initial question about encountering and overcoming challenges by reflecting oh how the labors, challenges, and experiences—both in the book and in their own lives—could lead to growth, even when the experiences were not necessarily "good." This also led to a discussion about how reflection on experiences can empower people to use their experiences for their growth.

In addition to the projects, the novel itself made a profound impact on some students who found themselves connecting to the experiences Hercules shared. Joclyn, a student who saw her father killed in her front yard a few years earlier, explained that it felt like the novel put her feelings into words for the first time since his death. Although not every student in Kaylee's class connected as closely to the text as Joclyn, the study of the original labors of Hercules and the Classical Mythology Application Projects gave students an authentic purpose for reading that many had not experienced before. Their projects allowed them to integrate their interests into their study of the text and to identify valuable connections to their own lives and the lives of their peers.

Considerations

Integrating dialogical strategies throughout unit-long inquiries created powerful opportunities for content-rich instruction centered on engaging texts. These inquiries involved a variety of intertextual experiences and various forms of classroom talk that fostered relatedness, autonomy, and sociality among students. Whether they take the form of whole-class-focused units like the ones created by Jeanie and JC, or more student-driven units like the one Kaylee designed, numerous opportunities exist to engage students in dialogical learning experiences.

In addition to those featured in this chapter, a variety of other stimulating tasks can generate situational interest throughout units. For example, the tableaus Mercedes's students created in Chapter 4 helped them gather evidence and draft questions for a mock trial where they tried Daisy for the murder of Myrtle Wilson. Jeanie wondered what kind of projects students might create in their own community after reading and studying the young reader's edition of William Kamkwamba's life in *The Boy Who Harnessed the Wind*. Both modern and classic transcendentalist texts could inspire students to design and embark on their own transcendental experiences.

The three teachers in this chapter each emphasized the importance of discussion and reflection to help students see clear correlations between the dialogical strategies and the readings. When this happened, students didn't just go through the motions of school—they learned through doing and felt emotions about their learning. Tasting the cacao, completing the labors, ducking and covering to the sound of the sirens—these experiences and others helped students live through the text. Like Carla Hannaford (1995) explained, when education is just an intellectual exercise, it falls short of the kind of learning, thinking, and creating possible through emotion and sensory experiences. The more attachment students felt to the experiences they read about, the more motivated they seemed to engage in the work of reading and writing.

These strategies also provided learning spaces for students to explore questions, conflicts, and the challenges of real life, but in spaces where it's safe to fail. JC explained that he saw these strategies as tools to help students engage with and imitate concepts, then to play with these ideas alongside their peers and teachers in ways that allowed them to digest the ideas and make them their own. Experiencing these situations helped students process and perform with their peers rather than just mentally take in information and spit it back out.

Although a myriad of possibilities exist for integrating dialogical strategies throughout entire units, it's important for teachers to be strategic. As she reflected on her unit, Jeanie explained,

Learning is messy, to really give them the experiences you are cracking eggs and messing up bowls. It's a lot of work and we can't do it every unit. But, for the things that matter, these strategies make the reading pop and make them remember.

Facilitating this kind of learning every day in every unit will likely exhaust both teacher and students. But students don't need big experiences every day; peppering them throughout the year or unit will suffice. Creating big learning moments that celebrate the inquiries teachers and students value helps the learning take on personal relevance and make a lasting impression.

References

Applebee, A., Langer, J., Nystrand, M., & Gamoran, A. (2003). Discussion-based approaches to developing understanding: Classroom instruction and student performance in middle and high school English. *American Educational Research Journal, 40*(3), 685–730.

Aronson, E. (2002). Building empathy, compassion, and achievement in the jigsaw classroom. In J. Aronson (Ed.) *Improving academic achievement: Impact of psychological factors on education* (pp. 209–225). Academic Press.

Beers, K. (2002). *When kids can't read: What teachers can do*. Heinemann.

Daniels, H. (2011). *Texts and lessons for content-area reading*. Heinemann.

Dean, D. (2021). *What works in writing instruction: Research and practice*, 2nd ed. NCTE.

Douglass J. & Guthrie, J. (2008). Meaning is motivating: Classroom goal structures. In J. Guthrie (Ed.) *Engaging adolescents in reading* (pp. 17–32). Corwin.

Frankel, J. (1975). Learning centers for reading in junior high. *Journal of Reading, 19*(3), 243–246.

Guthrie, J. (2008). *Engaging adolescents in reading*. Corwin.

Guthrie, J., Wigfield, A., Humenick, N., Perencevich, K., Taboada, A., & Barbosa, P. (2006). Influence of stimulating tasks on reading motivation and comprehension. *The Journal of Educational Research, 99*(4), 232–245.

Hannaford, C. (1995). *Smart moves: Why learning is not all in your head.* Great Ocean Publishers.

Harvey, M., Deuel, A., & Marlatt, R. (2019). "To be or not to be": Modernizing Shakespeare with multimodal learning stations. *Journal of Adolescent & Adult Literacy,* 63(5), 559–568.

Juzwik, M., Borsheim-Black, C., Caughlan, S. & Heinz, A. (2013). *Inspiring dialogue: Talking to learn in the English classroom.* Teachers College Press.

Middleton, R., Calonius, L., Lambert, D., United States Office of Civil Defense, C., National Education Association of the United States, C. & Castle Films, I. (1952). *Duck and cover.* Langlois, L. & Carr, L., comps, Archer Production Company, prod United States; Castle Films. [Video]. Retrieved from the Library of Congress, https://www.loc.gov/item/2022604365/

Movitz, A. & Holmes, K. (2007). Finding center: How learning centers evolved in a secondary, student-centered classroom. *English Journal,* 96(3), 68–73.

Pho, D. H., Nguyen, H. T., Nguyen, H. M., & Nguyen, T. T. N. (2021). The use of learning station method according to competency development for elementary students in Vietnam. *Cogent Education,* 8(1), 1870799.

Schmidt, G. (2023). *The labors of Hercules Beal.* HarperCollins.

Wellerstein, A. (2018). *Outrider.* [Interactive map and simulation]. Outrider.com. https://outrider.org/nuclear-weapons/interactive/bomb-blast

Wessling, S. (2024, May 16). *Conver-stations: A discussion strategy [Video]. The Teaching Channel* https://learn.teachingchannel.com/video/conver-stations-strategy

6

Continuing the Dialogue

One snowy, February Friday while writing this book, I received a text message from my 12-year-old nephew Luke. I'm his aunt so I might be partial, but I think he's a pretty smart kid. He does well in school and happens to be the all-time leading scorer in his middle school's Quidditch club, which keeps him busy and out of trouble in the basketball off-season. I've never met another human with a more encyclopedia-like knowledge of basketball and even though he's more interested in analyzing basketball plays than literature, he likes school. He's also thoughtful because he occasionally checks on his aunt, hence our text exchange on a wintery afternoon that went something like this:

Luke: how was your day?
Me: It's been pretty good—just lots of meetings and grading papers. How was your day? Are you done with school yet?
Luke: I got out already—at 3:07. My day was ok.
Me: Anything specific or just generally lame?
Luke: My classes, the things we did today were boring.

We continued our back-and-forth as he told me about his classes. One was "fine" because the teacher didn't make them do anything. Another one was "okay" because he had some friends in it. In English he didn't get to read anything fun. As he described his day, I couldn't help but recall a few lines from a John Steinbeck (2002) essay called "Like Captured Fireflies," where he wrote:

> It is customary for adults to forget how hard and dull and long school is. The learning by memory all the basic things one must know is the most incredible and unending effort. Learning to read is probably the most difficult and revolutionary thing that happens to the human brain and if you don't believe that, watch an illiterate adult try to do it.

Reading is hard work—and it's not just John Steinbeck and Luke who think so. Recent statistics also show this and although they varied slightly by source, each painted a similar picture. A recent College Board announcement declared American College Testing (ACT) scores fell nationwide for the sixth consecutive year, reflecting decreases in students' reading abilities in all subjects (ACT, 2023). National Assessment of Educational Progress (NAEP) shared similar stats, stating between only a quarter and one half of 8th grade students read at or above a proficient level across the disciplines (NAEP, 2022).

Interestingly—and this is where we get back to Luke—NAEP analyses correlated reading for fun with higher scores. Students who read for fun did better than students who received below-basic scores. This might seem like good news, but the trouble is, the number of students reading for pleasure continues to drop. In 2020 middle school pleasure reading fell to an all-time low, with only 17% of students reading for fun almost every day, 54% less than once or twice a week, and 29% never or hardly ever (Schaeffer, 2021). Stats were slightly higher for high school students, at 19%, 55%, 27% respectively. But these percentages reflect declines across the board for all races and ethnicities, with the lowest percentages among Black and Hispanic students. The numbers point to a few common issues that Steinbeck identified back in 1955 when he wrote his essay—that is, reading requires serious brain work, learning isn't easy, and schools often don't make it any easier by focusing primarily on facts and forgetting the fun.

But Steinbeck wasn't just waving the red flag; he also described the answer to this dilemma. In this same essay he wrote the following lines, lines that follow those I quoted earlier:

> School is not easy, and it is not for the most part very fun, but then if you are very lucky, you may find a teacher. (p. 00)

My nephew Luke (and countless other teens) agree with the part about school not being easy or very much fun. But you don't have to be John Steinbeck or a 7th grader to realize—or remember—the power of a teacher. Good teachers make all the difference.

In Luke's case, the exception to the boredom came in science with his biology teacher who asked the students to fill out brackets for "March Mammal Madness." This teacher caught basketball-loving Luke's attention with the word "bracket," then held him captive with a task only vaguely related to March Madness. In March Mammal Madness mammals from around the world face off in head-to-head comparisons of their strengths, weaknesses, and contributions to the planet.

I don't know Luke's teacher and I'm working only with a 7th grader's description of the activity, but it sounds like a hand-on, intertextual experience that rouses students' curiosity and invites questions that drive students to texts, discussions, and argumentation as they share evidence and synthesize their learning.

In short, it's dialogical.

I suspect Steinbeck would have supported dialogical approaches to teaching reading and literature because of the way he goes on to describe what made his own best teachers so great. For him, they shared these three characteristics:

> They all loved what they were doing. They did not tell—they catalyzed a burning desire to know. Under their influence, the horizon sprung wide and fear went away and the unknown became knowable. But most important of all, the truth, that dangerous stuff, became beautiful and very precious.
>
> (p. 142)

They loved teaching. They catalyzed a burning desire to know and made learning accessible. And precious truths became clear—all because of the way teachers invited learning.

Teachers face intense pressures from all angles and I am amazed at how so many do so much good for students as they continue to navigate ever-changing terrain. The teachers in this book exemplify the efforts of the countless great teachers across the nation who—despite standards, curricular expectations, and mandates—find ways to love what they do, to inspire student-driven inquiry, and to help students discover the importance of literacy, language, and learning.

The goal of this book has been to highlight strategies and approaches that put students in dialogue with books, one another, and the world around them. In addition to descriptions and research-based rationales, I included illustrations of teachers implementing these approaches in their own classrooms. I believe the way Steinbeck characterized his best teachers mirrors the characteristics of dialogical teachers. In this final chapter I use the three characteristics Steinbeck described to consider the power of dialogical approaches to teaching literature and reading to ignite powerful learning and then to explore recommendations to make this happen.

Love Teaching Reading, Literature, and Teens

Some teachers choose this career because they love teaching kids, some because they love teaching reading, some because they love teaching literature, and some a combination of all three. But regardless of which reason serves as the primary motive, it's imperative that teachers communicate that love to students. The school lives of students and teachers are often overflowing with paperwork, extracurricular activities, school politics, and jam-packed schedules. Sometimes these demands eclipse the joy of teaching, and we forget it was our love of reading, literature, and teenagers that originally drove us to this profession.

Perhaps that's why I appreciated my friend and colleague Chris Crowe who, when speaking to a movie theater full of literature-loving ELA and reading teachers, explained that the way teachers approach reading and literature instruction impacts our students for years to come. Quoting from William Wordsworth's "The Prelude," Chris reminded us that "What we have loved/others will love, and we will teach them how." Then he asked,

> We got into teaching because of our desire to help young people learn to love what we love. But what is it we love, exactly?...Unfortunately, because of our sophisticated adult involvement with literature, too many of us have forgotten the simple magic of reading. In our efforts to help students love what we love—literature—we overlook the more primary and very important task of helping them learn to love reading. Without an appreciation of and affection for the magic of reading, our students will never, ever gain a love of literature.
>
> (Crowe, 2024)

When I heard Chris emphasize a love of reading as the path to developing a love of literature, it reaffirmed to me the importance of the dialogical approaches utilized by the teachers featured in this book. Whether they taught "Capital L Literature" like *The Great Gatsby* or *Romeo and Juliet* from the traditional, but highly contested canon; or contemporary classics like *The Joy Luck Club* that enjoy a wide audience; or more popular YA texts with literary merit, such as novels like *The Serpent King*, nonfiction such as *There is No Ham in Hamburgers*, or graphic novels like *Bomb*, utilizing dialogical strategies helped these teachers show their students why reading mattered and helped them access emotions, experiences, feelings, and ideas that invited students to cultivate their love of the literature.

The teachers who participated in these dialogical experiences each loved their jobs, but they'd also each been teaching long enough to know teaching can be hard. Their years of experience ranged from less than three to over ten years, from rural classrooms in forgotten parts of the country to suburban and urban areas with diversity in language, culture, race, ability, and experience. The challenges and the mandates they faced mirrored those across the country. Kara and Kaylee worked with seniors facing a myriad of challenges from first-generation triumphs to students working to succeed amidst the challenges that addictions, teen pregnancies, and poverty pose for teens. Jeanie, Abby S., and Mercedes all worked to accommodate and create space for the diversity of languages and learners entering their schools and communities. Abby M.'s school expected common assessments among grade-level teams; Marion's students wondered about the rigor of anything that appeared to veer from traditional lecture and note taking; and Matti worked to close the gap for middle schoolers wrestling with reading and writing challenges.

As they reported their successes and challenges implementing these strategies in their classrooms, I was inspired by their creativity and ingenuity, but not surprised. Watching how Madison interweaved poetry analysis with soundscapes or how Abby used prop box artifacts to engage students in character analyses reminded me of both the potential for rigorous learning and the engagement fostered by dialogical strategies. JC, Kaylee, and Jeanie each used multiple strategies across units in combinations that captured the interests of students. Unprompted and uncorroborated, almost every single one of these teachers mentioned how utilizing dialogical strategies energized their teaching and reminded them why they got into teaching—because of their love of reading and learning.

Catalyze a Burning Desire to Know and Make Reading Accessible

Steinbeck's statement that the best teachers catalyzed in him "a burning desire to know" seemed to me the ideal definition of what it meant to facilitate authentic inquiry. Inquiry means to ask questions, to seek solutions, to discover answers. But how exactly do teachers light this flame in students?

Steinbeck uses the word "catalyst" in his explanation, and this seems to be the secret. In chemistry a catalyst changes conditions just enough to initiate a reaction that wouldn't happen otherwise. In reading, stimulating tasks serve as catalysts that change the level of student interest from "nonexistent" or "minimal" to "situational." In other words, stimulating tasks are catalysts that create temporary states of situational interest that motivate students to engage in inquiry and to learn something they might not otherwise find interesting. In some studies, the situational interest created by a stimulating task led to 10 hours of engaged reading as students raised questions and looked for answers together (Guthrie et al., 2006). The artifactual inquiries, simulations, and enactments described here all serve as powerful intertextual experiences that qualify as stimulating tasks—engaging, hands-on learning experiences that encourage students to think in new ways and generate situational interest in reading.

Part of the catalytic power of these strategies resides in the way they encourage and value the use of intertextuality as a way of exploring questions. Whether that means diving into written, oral, or digital texts like Jeanie's students did as they shared their food stories and traditions; participating in hands-on explorations like Matti's shoebox autobiographies; sharing experiences among class members like Abby S.'s banned books simulation; or drawing on generalizations from students' individual and collective lived experiences when students in Mercedes' classes weighed the choices facing the characters in their novel as well as ones in their own lives, these intertextual experiences served as stimulating tasks that helped students want to learn and to experience the issues in the text. Students saw firsthand the importance of dialoguing with texts and wrestling with issues.

The other part of the power lies in the questions themselves. Participating in stimulating tasks often leads students to generate questions they want to explore. Stimulating tasks give students experiences that help them want to learn and experience for themselves why it's important to dialogue with texts and wrestle with issues. They answer some of these through the exploration and sharing of intertextual experiences, but their questions also drive them to dialogue with texts, with their peers, and with the world around them. Teachers don't need to tell students what they are reading and learning is important when they are inspiring students to read and learn.

Make Truth Beautiful and Precious

Steinbeck isn't exaggerating. Learning and dialogue—as well as learning through dialogue—is increasingly fraught with peril. We live in an era where stakeholders across the political spectrum are vying for control to define what constitutes "truth," rather than engaging with one another in the search for it. But a quote from Bakhtin (1984) that I shared in Chapter 1 speaks to this quest for truth and the necessity of dialogue as a part of it. He explained, "Truth is not born nor is it to be found inside the head of an individual person, it is born between people collectively searching for truth, in the process of their dialogic interaction" (p. 110). The truth—and our understanding of it—results from our dialogical interactions with those learning alongside us, those writing what we are reading, those sharing the world we live in, and those on all sides of the issues. In other words, "truth" comes through dialogue.

Embedded in the dialogical strategies featured here are opportunities for formative, exploratory discussions where students ask questions of themselves and of one another. In these dialogues they consider multiple perspectives on issues and what an experience might feel like through the lens of the other. For example, JC's draft simulation put students in the shoes of young men facing the threat of war, Kara's students shared paper bag collages and learned what it meant to make assumptions about others based on external characteristics, and Marion's students participated in Conversations with Strangers to see the impact of point of view.

In addition, dialogical strategies also invite students to take positions on issues as they consider evidence, provide rationales for their arguments, and reason with one another. Marion's use of time capsules engaged students in analyses and discussions of historic documents and her explorations of a character's point of view helped students make arguments as they analyzed the connection between character's choices and the ultimate outcome of the plot. Similarly, Madison's soundscape and reader's theater became tools to help students identify evidence they could use to make arguments about themes and imagery; and Abby's book banning simulation inspired students to debate and defend their right to read, identifying evidence and considering audience as they began to craft their arguments.

Ultimately reflective discussions helped link students' experiences to the concepts, ideas, characters, and conflicts at the heart of their inquiries. No simulation would be complete without unpacking of the experience to explore parallels between real life and the text. Reflecting on dramatic strategies helped students recognize the empathy they felt for others as well as the way these wrestles played out in their own lives. And, providing space for students to consider the personal implications of experiences like Kara's letters from home activity and Matti's reader identity museum exhibit invited students to consider how learning experiences changed them.

These kinds of dialogues make the unknown knowable for all students, but particularly those who struggle with reading and those with learning disabilities. These strategies also appeal to those who often find themselves on the margins because their cultural or home experiences don't always match the traditional curriculum. In each of these instances, dialogical strategies make reading accessible and worthwhile for all students.

So Now What?

If these components characterize dialogical teaching and learning experiences that lead to engaged reading and rewarding learning for teachers and students, then the question that follows for coaches, administrators, and teacher educators should be "How can we help teachers do this?" Or for teachers, "What do these ideas mean for me and my students in my classroom?" and "How will these ideas shape my pedagogy?" The descriptions of how these teachers integrated dialogical approaches to teaching reading and literature into their classrooms offer ideas to spark your imagination as you consider the role of dialogical strategies in your own curriculum, but implementing dialogical strategies requires adaptations for the unique contexts of your own students, classrooms, curriculum, and communities. While you consider these factors, I'd offer these four recommendations:

Begin with High-Quality Texts that Require the Application of Disciplinary Reading Skills

As we brainstormed and planned, my first question to these teachers was something like "So what literature are you teaching this year?" To be clear, a truly student-driven dialogical approach would likely start with an invitation like "Tell me about your students" or "What kind of inquiry question would your class like to explore?" These questions shaped Jeanie and Kara's choice of texts and helped make the reading relevant for their students. But the realities of teaching often mean teachers are assigned books or given a list of approved books to teach and common assessments to go with them. As a result, crafting an inquiry often begins with a text.

If this starting point sounds familiar to you, you're not alone. Mercedes, Madison, Abby, and others faced similar situations as we considered their options. A high-quality text that requires the application of disciplinary reading skills is a key feature of content-rich instruction. The text might be a well-written, high-interest book that excites students, or it might be one that students don't even know exists. It could be a classic or something contemporary, from a scientific journal to a high-interest trade book written for young adults. There are tremendous advantages in using texts students already find appealing and that align with their interests, but high-quality texts at students' instructional level require them to use dialogic reading strategies to make sense of the text and get them talking.

Identify a Stimulating Task Linked to the Heart of the Inquiry

After narrowing down the text options, brainstorm a list of potential inquiry questions related to the text that might appeal to students. These are questions that invite them to explore connections and disconnections between the text and their own lives, to draw on their own cultures, interests, and perspectives to add texture and meaning to the exploration of the inquiry.

Thus far this approach to planning may not sound much different than any other literature unit. But it's at this juncture that it begins to diverge. After identifying inquiry questions, brainstorm possible intertextual experiences that invite students into the inquiry. How might artifacts, dramatic strategies, experiences, or simulations provide a catalyst for this inquiry? What might capture students' interests and inspire authentic questions? For example, what kind of simulation might help students wrestle with the conflicts at the heart of the novel? Or, what kinds of artifacts represent themes and symbols worth exploring and expand students' understanding of these ideas? How might stations introduce background knowledge, conflicts, or other information that will make the inquiry relevant, engaging, and inviting?

Begin with the end in mind and consider your goals for the end of the inquiry. Madison and Abby had very focused assessments, in some cases assessments already aligned with standards chosen for them and created by their teams. As they contemplated strategies they might use, they considered these factors as well and selected those that helped them reach these predetermined standards and prepare students for the assessments. For example, soundscapes provided a natural way to draw attention to sound imagery, mood, and tone and reader's theater helped students attend to nuances and details in the text. Prop boxes offered concrete ways to track abstract symbols, themes, and characterization.

Even if you're a teacher with more flexibility, it's important to think about how the stimulating task might support your assessments. In some instances, the dialogical strategies here focused on a lesson or two, but they also initiated dialogue throughout the unit and with the final assessment. Consider the way Kaylee's mythology application project provided an end goal for students' analysis and reflection on the myths and challenges in the novel as well as an opportunity for them to explore themes and use what they learned to re-imagine the challenges in their own lives. Or consider Kara's letters from home activity and the way students' experiences with their letters shaped their reading of the text and their ultimate analyses of the characters' experiences.

Also, consider the ways in which the stimulating task might provide an intertextual resource for students to make sense of the reading. As JC's students read the rest of the novel, they continued to refer to the draft simulation, putting themselves in the places of the characters. The discussions Jeanie embedded throughout her class's study of the chocolate chapter drew on their own family food traditions, their unique and collective cultural heritage, and their own stories. Multilingual students shared their expert knowledge of cultures and other students became experts as their content knowledge from other subjects was valued in language arts. In each of these instances the dialogical strategy offered a shared experience that drew from students' collective knowledge and helped the whole class make sense of the text.

We considered the approaches available and the inquiry questions that fit with the texts, piecing them together almost like a puzzle. Sometimes multiple pieces could fit; sometimes no matter how hard we tried to tweak a strategy, it just didn't fit right. Most of the time one approach provided the best fit for the text and the passion of the teacher.

Embed Routines and Frameworks that Require Reading and Get Students Talking

Once students get excited about the inquiry, they tend to ask questions and want answers. This is the prime time to harness the power of a stimulating task and to help them use the text to find answers to their questions. But rarely did these teachers just turn the reading over to the students to do on their own. Instead, they utilized approaches to reading that got students into the text together and got them talking.

Reciprocal teaching, embedded question protocols, and collaborative reasoning represent just a few frameworks that helped these teachers facilitate student discussion and argument within the class. The linchpin of dialogical strategies is dialogue with one another where students engage in open, free exchanges of ideas that involve their voices. Students' posing genuine questions and teachers building on students' comments supports and guides their learning.

For example, reciprocal teaching forced students to slow down and read together, ask questions, make predictions, summarize, and clarify the text. As they read and talked together, they co-constructed meaning and wrestled with questions they might have otherwise ignored. When paired with reader's theater and other dramatic strategies that put the responsibility of reading on the students, it engaged them in closer readings and discussions of the texts than would have happened if they read on their own.

In other instances, reading informally in small groups or pairs helped students pause to summarize, explore vocabulary, and make explicit connections between the text and characters as they engaged in during Good Angel, Bad Angel discussions or Conversations with Strangers. Then students revisited the text, read critically, and prepared more intentionally to share evidence to support their understandings. As they encountered different perspectives, they worked together to make sense of text and come to understandings and reconcile conflicting viewpoints or interpretations.

Include Opportunities for Metacognitive Thinking and Reflection

Metacognition and reflection provide the final, but essential elements of crafting dialogical strategies. Multiple examples included teachers modeling necessary skills and practices, such as the way Jeanie modeled and scaffolded the use of hands-on experiences throughout her class's study of the chocolate chapter before students read and researched their own chapters in the book. Marion normalized skepticism and a quizzical consideration of one another's motives in the "Who's the Witch?" simulation.

In these and almost every other instance, students benefited from explicit teaching, modeling, and then opportunities to imitate skills or practices central to the concepts taught. At some point the teacher made explicit the purpose of the intertextual experience and its connection to the reading. Students had opportunities to do their own connecting and reflecting about these connections, then their thinking became visible to each other through discussion. Stimulating tasks are just fun activities if students don't see how the task connects to the text and its ultimate purpose in supporting the reading and learning. This can be the easiest part to forget because it sometimes comes as the final element of planning or at the end of class when time runs short. But it's often the most essential part of lasting learning and the most important not to overlook.

These considerations don't address all the questions or possibilities for dialogical strategies. Questions I want to consider further include: What other types of intertextual experiences might work as stimulating tasks to engage students' interest and launch inquiry? Do multiple experiences of situational interest help adolescents develop sustained interest in reading? How do we know? What other reading and discussion strategies might be effectively integrated to provide opportunities for discussion and argument around an inquiry? Like all dialogues, more remains for others to contribute, challenge, and explore.

Conclusion

The dialogical approach to teaching reading and literature that I'm advocating for isn't so much a formula as a philosophy of practice that integrates rigorous, research-based practices with research on motivation and dialogical pedagogies. Bringing pieces together proves essential because even though we, as teachers, may love reading and the literature we teach, our students reside at the heart of the learning. Students like Travis, the 9th grader in rural Georgia who didn't feel feelings for words. Students like my nephew Luke, who like school, but like other things more, things that can easily be a part of the classroom conversation if teachers make space for them. Students like the kids in Kaylee's class who don't like reading or see connections among themselves, but who let a novel help them bridge gaps between people, break down barriers, and empathize with one another. This is what experiential strategies do—they help us consider the themes, characters, conflicts, and ideas in a text as a lens to view the world and one another differently.

Despite the somewhat discouraging reading stats and the perils of the modern classroom, most teachers I know went into teaching because the potential of creating these kinds of learning experiences excited them, because they enjoyed working with teens, and because they loved exploring questions related to the world and their content areas. Because they, like Lieutenant Colonel Hupfer, wanted to help their students learn to shoulder the challenges of a lifetime and to understand that reading empowers and opens possibilities. They wanted to be the kind of teachers Steinbeck described. To me, dialogical strategies and approaches offer tools to help teachers achieve these goals.

Steinbeck (2002) closed his essay by explaining:

> I have had many teachers who told me soon-forgotten facts but only three who created in me a new thing, a new attitude and a new hunger...I can tell my son who looks forward with horror to fifteen years of drudgery that somewhere in the dusky dark a magic may happen that will light up the years...if he is very lucky.
>
> (p. 143)

The act of reading and the literature we teach are both too important to be relegated to the category of "drudgery" by our students. There's never been more need and more opportunity to foster this attitude and hunger in our students as we prepare them to participate in the dialogues that will shape their lives and our communities. Dialogical strategies for teaching reading and literature can help to light up the years, for us and for our students. But intentional implementation of dialogical strategies means students aren't relying on luck to put them in the path of great teachers; instead, they maximize every students' opportunity to receive engaging and effective reading instruction.

References

ACT (2023, October 10). *Fewer high school seniors ready for college as ACT scores continue to decline.* ACT. https://leadershipblog.act.org/2023/10/act-scores-decline.html

Bakhtin, M. (1984). *Problems of Dostoevsky's poetics*. (C. Emerson, Trans). University of Michigan Press.

Crowe, C. (2024, February 2). *Helping students love to read* [Keynote presentation]. Annual Conference of the Utah Council of Teachers of English. Sandy, Utah, United States.

Guthrie, J., Wigfield, A., Humenick, N., Perencevich, K., Taboada, A., & Barbosa, P. (2006). Influence of stimulating tasks on reading motivation and comprehension. *The Journal of Educational Research*, *99*(4), 232–245.

National Assessment of Educational Progress (2022). U.S. Department of Education. Institute of Education Sciences, National Center for Education Statistics, National Assessment of Educational Progress (NAEP), 2022 Reading Assessment. United States.

Schaeffer, K. (2021, November 12). Among many US children, reading for fun has become less common, federal data shows. *Pew Research Center*. https://www.pewresearch.org/short-reads/2021/11/12/among-many-u-s-children-reading-for-fun-has-become-less-common-federal-data-shows/

Steinbeck, J. (2002). …like captured fireflies. In J. J. Benson *America and American: Selected nonfiction* (pp. 142–143). Penguin Putnam.

Appendix
Texts Mentioned

Acevedo, E. (2022). *Clap Where You Land*. Quill Tree.
Acevedo, E. (2018). *The Poet X*. HarperCollins.
Acevedo, E. (2019). *With the Fire on High*. HarperCollins.
Alexander, K. (2014). *The Crossover*. HMH.
Alexie, S. (2013). "Because My Father Always Said He Was the Only Indian Who Saw Jimi Hendrix Play 'The Star-Spangled Banner' at Woodstock." *The Lone Ranger and Tonto Fistfight in Heaven*. 20th Anniversary Edition. Grove Press.
Alvarez, Julia. (1992). "Snow." *How the García Girls Lost Their Accents*. Plume.
Anderson, L. (2002). *Fever, 1793*. Simon & Schuster.
Anderson, L. (1999). *Speak*. Penguin.
Atwood, K. (2018). *Courageous Women of the Vietnam War: Medics, Journalists, Survivors and More*. Chicago.
Auden, W. H. & Mendelson, E. (1995). "O What Is That Sound?" *Poems*. Knopf/Random House.
Austen, J. (1995). *Pride and Prejudice*. Dover.
Berry, J. (2019). *Lovely War*. Viking.
Bierce, A. (2008). "An Occurrence at Owl Creek Bridge." *An Occurrence at Owl Creek Bridge and Other Stories*. Dover Publications.
Boulley, A. (2021). *Firekeeper's Daughter*. Holt.
Bradbury, R. (1992). *Fahrenheit 451*. Del Rey.
Bradbury, R. (2010). "All Summers in a Day." *The Stories of Ray Bradbury*. Everyman's Library.
Burg. A. (2009). *All the Broken Pieces*. Scholastic.
Chase, P. (2019). *Dough Boys*. Greenwillow.
Chee, T. (2020). *We Are Not Free*. Clarion.
Chbosky, S. (2009). *The Perks of Being a Wallflower*. Pocket Books.
Christie, A. (2003). *And Then There Were None*. HarperCollins.

Cisneros, S. (1991). "Eleven." *Woman Hollering Creek, and Other Stories*. Random House.

Collins, S. (2008). *The Hunger Games*. Scholastic.

Crowe, C. (2014). *Death Coming Up the Hill*. Clarion.

Deschler, K. (2013). "The Hollow." *Poetry Soup*, https://www.poetrysoup.com/poem/the_hollow_502577. Retrieved 18 April 2024.

Dickens, C. (2012). *A Tale of Two Cities*. Penguin Classics.

Dobbs, A. (2021). *Barefoot Dreams of Petra Luna*. Sourcebooks.

Falkner, W. (2022). "A Rose for Emily." *A Rose for Emily and Other Stories*. Grapevine India Publishers.

Farmer, N. (2002). *House of the Scorpion*. Atheneum.

Fipps, L. (2021). *Starfish*. Nancy Paulsen.

Fitzgerald, F. (2019). *The Great Gatsby*. Wordsworth Editions.

Frank, A. (1989). *The Diary of Anne Frank*. Longman.

Gaiman, N., & James, M. (2020). "Click-Clack the Rattlebag." *The Neil Gaiman Reader: Selected Fiction*. First edition. HarperCollins Publishers.

Gillman, C. (2009). "The Yellow Wallpaper." *The Yellow Wallpaper and Selected Writings*. Little Brown UK.

Golding, W. (1954). *Lord of the Flies*. Perigee.

Gratz, A. (2021). *Ground Zero*. Scholastic.

Hansberry, L. (1997). *A Raisin in the Sun*. Random House.

Hawthorne, N. (2016). *The Scarlet Letter*. Penguin Classics.

Hemingway, E. (1927). "Hills like White Elephants." *Men Without Women*. Charles Scribner's Sons.

Hinton, S. E. (2016). *The Outsiders*. Penguin.

Hiranandani, V. (2024). *Amil and the After*. Kokila.

Huey, E. (2022). *Beneath the Wide Silk Sky*. Scholastic.

Hughs, K. (2020). *Displacement*. First Second.

Hugo, V. (2008). *Les Misérables* (J. Rose, Tran.; Modern Library edition). The Random House Publishing Group.

Irving, W. (2015). "The Legend of Sleepy Hollow." *The Legend of Sleepy Hollow and Other Tales*. Canterbury Classics.

Jacobs W. W. (2015). "The Monkey's Paw." (Pasden J., Ed.). Mind Spark Press.

Jackson, S. "The Lottery." *Literature: An Introduction to Fiction, Poetry, and Drama*. Harper Collins College Publishers, 1995.

Kamkwamba, W. & Mealer, B. (2016). *The Boy Who Harnessed the Wind: Young Reader's Edition*. Rocky Pond Books.

King, M. L., Jr. (2018). *Letter from Birmingham Jail*. Penguin Classics.

Konigsburg, E. (1996). *The View from Saturday*. Atheneum.
Knowles, J. (1988). *A Separate Peace*. Bantam Books.
Lai, T. (2011). *Inside Out and Back Again*. HarperCollins.
Latham, J. (2017). *Dreamland Burning*. Little Brown.
Lee, H. (2010). *To Kill a Mockingbird*. Arrow.
Lewis, J., Aydin, A. & Powell, N. (2013). *March*. Penguin.
Lo, M. (2021). *Last Night at the Telegraph Club*. Dutton.
Lockhart, E. (2014). *We Were Liars*. Delacorte.
Lowry, L. (1993). *The Giver*. HMH.
McBride, A. (2021). *Me Moth*. Macmillan.
McCall, G. (2012). *Summer of the Mariposas*. Lee & Low.
McManus, K. (2017). *One of Us Is Lying*. Delacorte.
Méndez, Y. (2020). *Furia*. Algonquin.
Messner, K. (2019). *Breakout*. Bloomsbury.
Miller, A. (2000). *The Crucible*. Penguin Classics.
Myers, W. (1998). *Fallen Angels*. Scholastic.
Myers, W. (2001). *Monster*. Amistad.
Niven, J. (2015). *All the Bright Places*. Ember.
O'Brien, T. (2009). *The Things They Carried*. HMH.
O'Connor, F. (2019). "A Good Man Is Hard to Find." *A Good Man Is Hard to Find*. Faber & Faber.
Orwell, G. (2021). *Nineteen Eighty-Four*. Penguin Classics.
Palacio, R. J. (2012). *Wonder*. Knopf.
Park, L. (2010). *A Long Walk to Water*. Clarion.
Partridge, E. (2018). *Boots on the Ground: America's War in Vietnam*. Viking.
Peña, M. (2010). *Mexican Whiteboy*. Random House.
Poe, E. (2004a). "The Cask of Amontillado." *The Tell-Tale Heart and Other Writings*. Bantam Classics.
Poe, E. (2004b). "The Raven." *The Tell-Tale Heart and Other Writings*. Bantam Classics.
Poe, E. (2004c). "The Tell-Tale Heart." *The Tell-Tale Heart and Other Writings*. Bantam Classics.
Powell, P. & Strickland, S. (2017). *Loving vs. Virginia*. Chronicle.
Reynolds, J. (2017). *Ghost*. Atheneum.
Reynolds, J. (2019). *Long Way Down*. Atheneum.
Rinaldi, A. (2002). *A Break with Charity: A Story About the Salem Witch Trials*. Clarion.
Rowling, J. K. (2007). *Harry Potter and the Deathly Hallows*. Scholastic.

Ryan, P. (2017). *Echo*. Scholastic.
Ryan, P. (2002). *Esperanza Rising*. Scholastic.
Sanchez, E. (2017). *I Am Not Your Perfect Mexican Daughter*. Knopf.
Satrapi, M. (2004). *Persepolis*. Pantheon.
Schmidt, G. (2023). *The Labors of Hercules Beal*. Harper Collins.
Schmidt, G. (2007). *The Wednesday Wars*. HMH.
Schneider, R. (2014). *The Beginning of Everything*. Katherine Tegen Books.
Schur, M. (1997). *Sacred Shadow*. Dial.
Schusterman, N. (2017). *Scythe*. Simon & Schuster.
Schusterman, N. (2007). *Unwind*. Simon & Schuster.
Sepetys, R. (2020). *Fountains of Silence*. Philomel.
Sepetys, R. (2023). *I Must Betray You*. Philomel.
Sepetys, R. (2017). *Salt to the Sea*. Philomel.
Shakespeare, W., & Brooks, H. F. (2009). *A Midsummer Night's Dream*. Bloomsbury Arden.
Shakespeare, W. (1992a). *Macbeth*. Wordsworth Editions.
Shakespeare, W. (1992b). *Othello* (C. Watts, Ed.). Wordsworth Editions.
Shakespeare, W. (1993). *Romeo and Juliet*. Dover Publications.
Shakespeare, W. (2000). *The Merchant of Venice* (C. Watts, Ed.). Wordsworth Editions.
Shakespeare, W. (1992c). *The Tragedy of Hamlet, Prince of Denmark* (New Folger's ed.). Pocket Books.
Sheinkin, S. & Bertozzi, N. (2023). *Bomb (Graphic Novel): The Race to Build—and Steal—the World's Most Dangerous Weapon*. Roaring Brook Press.
Sidman, J. (2010). *Dark Emperor and Other Poems of the Night*. Clarion.
Slater, D. (2017). *The 57 Bus*. Farrar, Straus & Giroux.
Smith, A. (2017). *The Way I Used to Be*. Margaret McElderry Books.
Smith, C. (2018). *Hearts Unbroken*. Candlewick.
Soto, G. (1991). "7th Grade." *Taking Sides*. San Diego, Harcourt Brace Jovanovich.
Speare, E. (1958). *The Witch of Blackbird Pond*. Clarion.
Steinbeck, J. (2000). *Of Mice and Men*. Penguin.
Steinbeck, J. (2017). *The Grapes of Wrath*. Penguin.
Stevenson, B. (2015). *Just Mercy*. One World.
Stockton, F. (1887). *The Lady, or the Tiger? and Other Short Stories*. New York, C. Scribner's sons. [Pdf] Retrieved from the Library of Congress, https://www.loc.gov/item/41031389/
Stone, N. (2017). *Dear Martin*. Crown.

Tahir, S. (2022). *All My Rage*. Penguin.

Tan, A. (2012). *The Joy Luck Club*. Penguin.

Thomas, A. (2017). *The Hate U Give*. Balzer + Bray.

Townley, A. (2019). *Captured: An American Prisoner of War in North Vietnam*. Scholastic.

Vizzini, N. (2007). *It's Kind of a Funny Story*. Disney-Hyperion.

Vonnegut, K. (2010). "Harrison Bergeron." *Welcome to the Monkey House: A Collection of Short Works*. Dial Press Trade Paperbacks.

Walsh, L. (2022). *Red Scare: A Graphic Novel*. Graphix.

Watson, R. (2017). *Piecing Me Together*. Bloomsbury.

Wharton, E. (1987). *Ethan Frome*. Penguin.

Wilde, O. (1973). *Importance of Being Earnest*. Avon Books.

Williams, A. (2019). *Genesis Begins Again*. Atheneum.

Woodson, J. (2016). *Brown Girl Dreaming*. Nancy Paulsen.

Yang, G. (2006). *American Born Chinese*. First Second.

Yousafzai, M. (2016). *I Am Malala*. Little Brown.

Zachman, K. & Donnelly, P. (2021). *There's No Ham in Hamburgers*. Running Press Kids.

Zentner, J. (2021). *In the Wild Light*. Random House.

Zentner, J. (2017). *The Serpent King*. Ember.

Zoboi, I. & Salaam, Y. (2020). *Punching the Air*. Balzer + Bray.

Zusak, M. (2007). *The Book Thief*. Knopf.

For Product Safety Concerns and Information please contact our EU
representative GPSR@taylorandfrancis.com
Taylor & Francis Verlag GmbH, Kaufingerstraße 24, 80331 München, Germany

www.ingramcontent.com/pod-product-compliance
Lightning Source LLC
Chambersburg PA
CBHW052340230426
43664CB00041B/2575